You, Inc.

Endorsements

"We live in times of unprecedented change, where what we do for a living is no longer separate from who we are and what we value. In *You, Inc.*, Rosie Bank presents network marketing not only as a business but as a way of life and a vehicle to fulfill one's life purpose. Done with this kind of wholeheartedness, any venture is bound to succeed. Rosie provides the treasure map for you to conquer your dreams. Start reading and get going, the world is waiting for the gift of *you*."
Josephine M. Gross, PhD, editor-in-chief *Networking Times*, dean of faculty, Networking University

"Way to go, Rosie. Thanks for choosing to make a difference and for helping all of us to know that we don't have to take life the way it comes to us. We can design life the way we want it … on our terms. This book is a must for anyone looking to find and live his or her best life."
Lynn Allen-Johnson, author, *Getting Out of Your Own Way*

"This book focuses on the key ingredient for success in owning a business: **YOU.** You only sell you. The decision of the buyer is based on the value of the seller. Value must be internalized, before it can materialize. Read, learn, and apply Rosie's principles and you will save months, even years, of trial and error as you network your way to the top."
Dr. Denis Waitley, author, *The Psychology of Winning*

"*You, Inc.* puts the power of our lives back in our hands! Too often we have been made to feel like victims, especially regarding our health. It is up to us to take control and realize the power within ourselves. *You, Inc.* gives you the courage and insight to take control of your life, maximize your time, and live a full, healthy life. Rosie Bank's approach, through research and her own life experience, creates a wonderfully powerful tool. Rosie not only talks about self-power, she lives it!"
Jennifer Azzi, Olympic gold medalist, international motivational speaker

"This book will quickly take you from frustration to success in building your own network marketing business. It is loaded with practical ideas to help you sell more and recruit faster than ever before."
Brian Tracy, author, *Maximum Achievement*

"Rosie Bank delivers powerful content in her amazing book *You, Inc.* Everyone would benefit from reading the truths found therein."
Robert G. Allen, best-selling author *Multiple Streams of Income*

"Rosie Bank is one who lives life to the fullest with a mentality of abundance. She recognizes the importance of giving back and supporting others. Within the pages of *You, Inc.*, Rosie generously shares her wisdom and expertise for all her readers to be inspired, educated, and uplifted. What a fantastic guide to generate massive momentum in your network marketing business."
Zachary Ross, co-founder, Larsen Global Alliance

"Rosie Bank has a huge heart and an incredible passion for helping others. Two things about her experience make this book a must read. First, what she has learned on her long journey of self-development is about the most insightful reflection you will ever come across. This will serve everyone who reads this book on *their* journey. Second, her success formula for aspiring network marketers is both hard earned and the real deal. Read the book. Take her wisdom to heart as you let your life and your business soar to higher levels by following her expert guidance."
Brian Klemmer, founder, Klemmer and Associates, author, *The Compassionate Samurai*

"Rosie has a blueprint for you that will guide you through your interior terrain. Owning your greatness and adjusting your beliefs and your self-image are the underpinnings of your ability to thrive and bring others along on the journey. Rosie has clearly done this work and continues to do so. If you will fall in step with her insightful tips and recommendations, you can expect life changing results as well. I would urge anyone in my own organization as well as anyone in network marketing to take this book to heart, and make a commitment to become the leader you were meant to be."
Ladd McNamara, MD, retired physician, full-time network marketer, author *The Cholesterol Conspiracy*

"Rosie Bank has done a masterful job taking what she has learned in the network marketing business and documenting it in her book, *You, Inc.* Her book is the next best thing to Rosie coaching you one-on-one. Anyone in network marketing could greatly benefit from the wisdom contained in this book."
Eric Lofholm, President Eric Lofholm International, author *How to Sell in the New Economy*

"Rosie Bank has written a remarkable book for anyone wondering how to harness the power of network marketing in creating their own financial security. Rosie has created a life of fulfillment and prosperity for herself and her family, and has done so with honesty and integrity, in a way that is accessible to everyone. With the country in financial turmoil, this book is a must-read for establishing freedom and financial independence."
Lloyd Watts, author, *The Flow of Time and Money: How to Create a Full and Prosperous Life*

"I highly recommend Rosie Bank's book *You, Inc.* She asks you to put the responsibility for your success squarely where it belongs—on you. She shares the wisdom of her many years as an entrepreneur and gives you a valuable step-by-step process for you to treat your business like a business and create the success you desire. This book is must read!"
Maureen G. Mulvaney, MGM, author, *The Women's Millionaire Club*

"Rosie Bank has delivered a well-rounded, no-nonsense recipe for success in network marketing. Just add her ingredients, keep stirring, and anyone can succeed! No fluff, no hype, no excuses. *You, Inc.* is a can-do formula chock full of ideas, inspiration, and insight. It puts control and accountability right where it belongs, in our own hands. Rosie is a person of great value, a dedicated leader, and passionate about her work. She knows her subject, and as a veteran entrepreneur she truly walks the walk. But even more importantly is her dedication to teach you to do the same."
Jenny Bisset, co-author, *Slender with a Blender*

"I urge everyone to buy a copy as soon as you can lay your hands on this. Rosie's book is beautifully written and executed. It is simple, yet specific. The words are written from a goddess of network marketing with wisdom, compassion, and integrity. This is a 'must read' by all incoming and seasoned associates."
Donna G. Barnett, Registered Nurse, professional network marketer, and originator of The Rhyming RN

"One thing rare in today's fast-paced world is to find someone who walks her talk. Rosie Bank does just that. In this book, *You, Inc.*, Rosie has written a solid handbook on the time-tested, fundamental principles of network marketing. If you're aiming to get to the top in this industry in any company, I recommend you read and re-read this book and use it as a training manual to guide your team to success. Rosie has written an exceptional book."
Ani Black, International Network Marketing Leader

Also by Rosie Bank
(As Rosie Spiegel)

Yoga for Rolfers, Movement Teachers, and Their Clients

Bodies, Health, and Consciousness

Lessons in Embodiment

You, Inc.

Own Your Business, Own Your Life through Network Marketing

ROSIE BANK

iUniverse, Inc.
New York   Bloomington

You, Inc.
Own Your Business, Own Your Life through Network Marketing

Copyright © 2010 Rosie Bank

All rights reserved. No part of this book may be used or reproduced by any means, graphic, electronic, or mechanical, including photocopying, recording, taping or by any information storage retrieval system without the written permission of the publisher except in the case of brief quotations embodied in critical articles and reviews.

Photography by George Wolga
Artwork by David Caggiano

iUniverse books may be ordered through booksellers or by contacting:

iUniverse
1663 Liberty Drive
Bloomington, IN 47403
www.iuniverse.com
1-800-Authors (1-800-288-4677)

Because of the dynamic nature of the Internet, any Web addresses or links contained in this book may have changed since publication and may no longer be valid. The views expressed in this work are solely those of the author and do not necessarily reflect the views of the publisher, and the publisher hereby disclaims any responsibility for them.

ISBN: 978-1-4502-3378-1 (sc)
ISBN: 978-1-4502-3380-4 (dj)
ISBN: 978-1-4502-3379-8 (ebk)

Library of Congress Control Number: 2010907916

Printed in the United States of America

iUniverse rev. date: 07/14/2010

For my parents

"Success is not to be pursued; it is to be attracted by the person you become."~ Jim Rohn, author, *How to Live a Successful Life*

"The more wealth a person has, the more likely that person will say, 'My success is a direct result of loving my career or business.'"~ Dr. Thomas Stanley, author, *The Millionaire Mind*

Contents

Foreword

∽

I know first-hand the positive impact a network marketing career can have on a family. Fifteen years ago, I was a single mother with a high school education, very limited business experience, and five children to support. Looking back on my situation, it seemed the timing to start a business could not have been worse. I've since learned that most opportunities come at inopportune times, so they are often misinterpreted as distractions. I started my network marketing business with the lofty goal of making enough income simply to pay for the nutritional products I needed for my family.

Today, through network marketing, I have achieved complete financial freedom. We now have the ability to go anywhere we want, and, in fact, we have traveled the world as a family. I work with people who lift me, people I respect and admire—like Rosie Bank. When I started my network marketing business fifteen years ago I hoped to make a difference in the lives of my children. I've since learned that our industry is all about making a difference in the world.

This book is entitled *You, Inc.*, but it is about much more than being your own boss. Within these pages, Rosie, my friend and colleague, teaches us truths about freedom, health, and joy and how network marketing can provide an ongoing means to those ends. As one who has had her life changed in every manner through network marketing, I feel honored and blessed to reflect on Rosie's determination to guide others.

As in any industry (teaching, aviation, nursing, engineering), there is a wide range of professionalism found among its advocates. For those of us who have made a career from network marketing, we believe that this is an honorable profession. Clearly, Rosie's intent to contribute for the purpose of raising the bar can help shed light for newcomers as well as seasoned distributors. Having someone out in front to lead the way can make a world of difference for anyone determined to succeed.

I have met, become friends with, and spent countless hours with many of the top leaders in this great industry. Those who are most determined to make their lives about helping others become leaders in their own right. What makes a leader is someone most committed to developing others. In this regard, both Rosie and this inspiring book will leave a legacy of people who will become happier, healthier, and more prosperous by benefiting from the wisdom offered so generously and so sincerely. This book will make a world of difference for anyone who reads it. But, as Rosie emphasizes, you must put what you learn in to practice. This is true of anything that has the power to change your life.

Rosie has drawn on her own life experiences in the fields of health and business not only to share her own story but to do so in a way that teaches principles critical to success in networking. That she teaches in a way so personal and genuine, so full of honesty, common sense, and practical application, is a gift to everyone who reads this book. Rosie's willingness to teach from her mistakes as well as from her successes makes this among the most genuine books on the subject. You, the reader, will be comforted to learn what we call "failing forward." Recently, when asked what she thought was the definition of failure, Rosie responded, "Not learning from our mistakes." Rosie's experiences are broad as well as deep. She has earned her stripes insofar as being highly qualified to communicate to you what it takes to be among the winners. The uniqueness of this book stems from the degree to which her disclosure, based on her own experience, can positively impact the results you can achieve.

I've watched Rosie carefully over the past ten years, and I'm certain her highest purpose is to inspire and enable those she works with to reach their own lofty and noble goals. When you find a strong and dedicated coach in network marketing, you will be encouraged in ways you have never experienced elsewhere in your life. If you will take the words on the following pages to heart, you will be that much closer to living what we call your best life. If you want to learn how to build a strong, profitable, and stable organization, you came to the right place.

Reading *You, Inc.* is your opportunity to embark on a personal and enlightening journey, one that has the power to transform all aspects of your life. We often hear that it is not only what you make in terms of financial gain that is the biggest prize in this industry. Who you become is its own reward. This book will tell you what to do. But more importantly, with the wisdom gained over many years in business for herself, Rosie will show you who to become. There are many excellent books on network marketing. But few, if any, provide such a clear guide for the inner work. Rosie shares with you the inside secrets that, when revealed, bring a refreshing feel to this work that will compel you to go the distance. Rosie is a treasure as a trusty guide. Many lives will be impacted by this book. Hopefully you will allow yours to be one of them.

Collette Larsen
Founder, Larsen Global Alliance

Preface

When my daughter, Octavia, was a little girl, she played with Barbie dolls, just as I did when I was her age. When girls play-act with their dolls, each doll gets a role. Octavia's Barbies always went to work to run their own corporations. They never had a job. They were always their own boss. Her Barbies were in charge of their lives. These were powerful dolls.

My children were born into a family of entrepreneurs. My father always owned his own company. He has been a role model of generosity and prosperity throughout my children's lives. In fact, what I have learned from my dad is sprinkled throughout this book.

To my son, Forest, and his sister, I have always been a business owner. They have seen me work hard and play hard. They know that when I am working, my office might be off limits. When they were younger, they knew that I could be laser-focused at times and could barely look up to give them what they needed. But this was more than made up for by the unhurried visits and quality time we got to spend together while other parents were away at their jobs.

My first career was launched prior to earning my undergraduate degree in 1975. For over thirty years I built and maintained a practice in body therapy and Rolfing, and I taught movement, yoga, and bodywork. This career took me all over the world, and I was blessed to have found a calling so early. I wrote books, gave talks and interviews, and facilitated groups and individuals throughout the United States and in Mexico. I founded SRG Publishing to promote my books and audio programs. It was a long and gratifying career. There were some speed bumps along the way, but I never needed or wanted to get a regular job. Working for myself was immensely satisfying, and I was quite happy. I believed wholeheartedly in the value of the craft in which I was trained and the service I provided to my clients and students.

My kids have never seen me get fired or laid off. They have never heard me complain about a boss or unfair wages. We have always vacationed when we wanted to. I never had to get permission to take a day off. And I was typically in my home office when they returned from school in the afternoon. I consider myself a messenger from the world of business ownership.

I look around at my home, my circle of friends, my lifestyle, my finances, and how my family and I have benefited from a series of choices that began in 1973. I feel blessed. Over the years, I have remained focused and disciplined, had a lot of fun, and grown immeasurably along the way. I have taken the bad with the good, had my teeth knocked out a couple of times, but never lost my determination to make it on my own. Some nights I was either too worried or too excited about my business to sleep. I do not need to paint a rosy picture, and I have nothing to prove. Simply, I am thrilled that I walked this path for what I have learned; for the teachers, colleagues, and friends who have inspired me; and for whom I have become.

My second and current career began in 1999. I am proud to say that I am a network marketer. I am in business for myself and work closely with other business owners who are my partners. We learn, grow, train, and travel together. We inspire one another and continually share resources to help each other prosper. Because the spirit and vision of our parent company is exceptional, we share a belief system that builds close bonds. We catch each other when we fall and provide incredible support that ensures that anyone determined to succeed will get exactly what she or he needs from the organization. I work with some of the most intelligent, professional, fun-loving, determined, and caring people I have ever known. I feel tremendous gratitude for finding a second calling. The only work I have ever done has been in the wellness field. I fell in love with nutrition the way I had fallen in love with yoga, movement, and body-oriented therapy.

During the year when this book was being written, the chaos in the global financial markets escaped no one's awareness. Just before the collapse of the stock market in September 2008, I heard a professional in the banking business say that the state of our finances reflects the state of our emotions. I doubt I am alone in having witnessed a series of events that looked like massive greed and fear eroding the bedrock of this country's economic stability.

What does all this have to do with network marketing? Thanks to our continuous cash flow from our network marketing businesses, those of us who stayed the course are experiencing on-going calm and predictability with regards to our finances. If you choose a solid company, the income you build is income that you own. I will never forget the first time I woke up to new commissions of more than one thousand dollars waiting for me in my business account *before* I went to work that week. I sat at my desk staring at my computer screen without blinking. I knew that this gift was the result of my inner work. I had to shift internally to allow myself to accept this treasure. The more I appreciated this gift, the greater the gift became. My new set of beliefs was up and running, and I was prepared to experience the abundance I had desired for a long time. Now my mission is to give back as much as possible.

My encouragement and enthusiasm are unbridled, notwithstanding the admission that the path of entrepreneurialism is not for everyone. If this motivates you to learn how to create and attract more freedom and joy along *your* chosen career path, I will be thrilled to have been a conduit for relaying this message. If my experience provides something for you to glean in order to shed light on your journey, I will know that this project has been a success. I am passionate about many things and excited about life. Sharing this information with others touches me deeply. Perhaps you are like me. You may look back one day at your choice to go into business for yourself and consider it among the best decisions of your life.

Rosie Bank

March 2010
Foster City, California

Acknowledgments

〜

T he way to complete a big project is to begin with the end in mind. The chance to thank the gifted, generous, and spectacular individuals whose contributions helped make this book great was the prize that awaited me since I began this venture.

I bow with gratitude, love, and thanks to Collette Larsen, for your friendship and endless mentoring and for the network marketing goddess that you are. Your belief in and contribution to this project kept me going from the beginning. To my teachers, Denis Waitley, Brian Klemmer, Brian Tracy, Eric Lofholm, and Robert Allen: thank you from the bottom of my heart for all you have taught me. Your work has changed my life, and your endorsements were dreams come true. To my friends and colleagues—Lynn Allen-Johnson, Dr. Ladd McNamara, Jennifer Azzi, Jenny Bisset, and Donna Barnett … thank you for your enthusiasm and for gracing this book with your inspiring words. To Zachary Ross, thank you for your infinite bigheartedness and wisdom, and for embodying the spirit of network marketing for anyone who is blessed to meet you. I offer a special thanks to Pete Zdanis, for your generously allowing me to find my written voice within our company through your world-class e-mail forum. To my friend and colleague, Dr. Lloyd Watts, for your contributions to this field that started with but now go way beyond this book. To Chris and Josephine Gross, for your support, encouragement, and breathtaking contribution to the industry of network marketing and to this project in particular: your work will cause ripples for a long time to come. To Maureen G. Mulvaney, for your unstoppable passion for helping others that continues to change lives. To Lucy Sanna, for your friendship, business partnership, and brilliance as an editor: these are gifts for which I am eternally grateful. To Ani Black, for receiving me on your doorstep where I landed when I was an infant in this industry, for raising me like your own, and for being an excellent guide along the way. To Duane Spears, thank you for helping me build a nest online to support this project. To Tammy and Tony Daum, for your encouragement and coaching that has made a world of difference. To J'en El, thank you for being out in front, shining the light for me with your love and encouragement. I owe a debt of gratitude to members of Manifesting Vision International; anyone who has a sizable organization knows that it takes a village to build and secure a team. Thank you to Dr. Myron Wentz, for your vision, leadership, and world-class products; and for the privilege of having found work that I would do tomorrow even if I won the lottery. I thank the team at iUniverse for your impeccable support and expert guidance in helping to turn my dream into a book.

I offer thanks and love from the bottom of my heart to my father, the greatest entrepreneur I have ever known; to my mother, for teaching me the value of frugality; my grown children, Forest and Octavia, for always encouraging my path of entrepreneurialism; and to Mark, my soon-to-be husband, for your editing and illustrating talents that helped to bring this project to completion, and for loving me and believing in me and in my mission in a way that helped me discover my greatness.

Part One
Getting Started

Introduction

Network marketing is a glorious industry. It is not for everybody, but when it is a good fit, the sky is the limit. I wrote this book in an earnest attempt to explain as much as I could about network marketing from my experience, in the hope that others may benefit from what I've learned.

You, Inc. is structured as a guide aimed toward achieving two goals:

- If you seek to profit from being your own boss, you may discover a pathway here to lead you to fulfilling your goals and dreams.
- If you come to network marketing as a skeptic, perhaps the experience and coaching offered in this book will help open your mind.

If you are considering network marketing for the first time, come in, relax, and stay a while. I wish I could invite you into my home, where we could sit down together, share a pot of tea, ask each other a million questions, and talk frankly about what you want in your life. *You, Inc.* is my attempt to do that with you.

Whether or not network marketing is for you, I hope that by the time you finish this book, you will be much clearer about your decision. Did you pick this book up feeling skeptical? We find in some instances the most skeptical people are protecting a part of their lives that is frankly not worth defending. If you discover that, indeed, some of the things you long for may be attainable by embracing this business model, it is in your best interest to be as open and honest with yourself as I will be with you. Just by asking yourself a new set of questions, you may realize that you can open doors that might otherwise be closed. Please don't be afraid to listen to your own desires. The courage you bring to examining your life could define what you are able to create from this moment forward.

When was the last time someone told you that he or she cared about the quality of your life and believed that you deserve to live that life? If you are ready for change, this might be music to your ears. If you question your ability to have a different and better life, this conversation might elicit self-doubt and disbelief. Either way, I am here to help you explore new possibilities.

For those of you who hear yourselves saying yes to the suggestions made in *You, Inc.*, I hope you will stay in this conversation. What starts as a cursory look could become a treasure of an opportunity for you and your loved ones. You can start by putting your toes into the water. Eventually, perhaps, you may find yourself easing into new ways to feel in control. What may become something that changes your life starts with the smallest of steps.

The first section of *You, Inc.* contains a series of stories and illustrations that serve as a road map. You will have the chance to look at your beliefs about what you are able to accomplish in your life. You may have a terrific life already. But if you have dreams and goals yet to be realized, ask yourself what you would change if you could. As much as I believe in and love this industry, I do not claim that a thriving network marketing business will solve all life's problems. You may be surprised, however, by how many limitations can be lifted through this model. If anything you read here pushes your buttons or causes you to feel resistance or disagreement, those might be the points where you have the most to learn. If you find yourself bubbling with desires and dreams in reading the pages to follow, this business may be just what you've been looking for. Also in this section, I include some health tips because I believe that taking good care of yourself ultimately affects your bottom line.

The chapter entitled "Treat Your Business like a Business" is a bit longer than the other chapters. I wanted to make sure that in addition to the inspiring stories and practical tips located elsewhere in *You, Inc.*, you would also gain clear and concise knowledge about what to do when you go to work on your networking business.

The second section of *You, Inc.* contains a collection of essays I published in *Networking Times Magazine* and the text of selected talks I have given. The compilation of quotes is a highlight of this section; this is the document I use over and over to help people appreciate the credibility and viability of network marketing. In this section you will also find exercises designed to further support you in seeing what you, yourself, can gain in embracing the philosophies found within this business model. Under "Recommended Reading and Listening," you will discover a collection of the work of some of the brightest minds in the arenas of business, network marketing, finance, health, leadership, and personal development. We say that readers are leaders and learners are earners. The resources listed are intended to guide you further, if you choose to embark on this path.

What do you have to lose by surrendering to the possibilities being offered to you? If you found a great company with high-quality products, would you recommend those products to other people? An affirmative answer to that question brings you one step closer to the golden ring called *freedom*. Can you imagine a life that has a greater emphasis on helping other people as you continue to invest in your own self-worth? If yes, then you are closer, still. And most importantly, what are the consequences of *not* taking action? Take your age and add five years to it. You will be that old in five years whether you get involved in network marketing or not. Who you will be in five years, and the quality of your life at that time, will be the result of decisions you make today, the friends you keep, the books you read, and the coaches you choose. If you find yourself thinking "too busy," "can't sell," "not enough time," or "this doesn't work," stop before you convince yourself of imagined limitations. I am extending a hand to you to step across the line. On this side all things are possible. No one deserves a better life more than you.

* * * * *

When I got involved with my current (and final) network marketing company in 1999, I was not new to the industry. Having failed with three previous companies, I swore I would never do it again. But I did. Here's why:

- I believed network marketing would support my values of leadership and personal development as career themes.
- My friend was trustworthy. He had what I wanted: a better way to make money and a system to work synergistically with other people.
- I had been practicing body therapy and teaching yoga for almost thirty years, and I was ready for a change. I was looking for something more stimulating and more intellectually challenging.
- My work was always about helping people to be healthier and to live more successfully in their bodies. Promoting the health benefits attainable through nutrition was a way to provide solutions for people to enjoy greater well-being than they were able to previously.
- The chance to grow professionally and to make a greater difference for others was irresistible. Because the core of this business model is to teach others about health and wellness, and to inspire them to inspire others, I felt I could touch more lives compared with what I had been doing before.

- People were making a lot of money in network marketing. I felt that the train had left the station and I wasn't on it. My income was linear, and I had to be present for each dollar that I made. I longed for a better way to be compensated financially.

My second career in the wellness industry came as a result of blending my love of nutrition and my love for being in business for myself. I came back to network marketing. Because of the culture and the values taught, I have learned to relax around time, health, and money. This has been worth the price of admission and has given me a huge desire to pay it forward. You will find among successful, dedicated network marketers a strong desire to inspire as many people as possible. In that regard, success begets success as we become more determined to help others improve *their* lives.

I have spent the last ten years in complete immersion. I have read more than three hundred books on network marketing, finance, leadership, personal development, nutrition, health promotion, and disease prevention. I have spent what would be months on end both attending and presenting seminars in person, via conference calls, and on the Internet. Since day one I agreed to be teachable, and I've worked diligently to create a solid organization.

Because I am hooked on helping people, I work my business tirelessly. Seizing opportunities for self-development has changed me as an entrepreneur and enabled me to do a better job of helping others change their lives. There have been teachers, mentors, and colleagues who believed in me, held me accountable, and became my friends. Brian Tracy says that you know if you are in the right field if you would still do what you do tomorrow even if you won the lottery. Many of us in network marketing feel that way, including those of us who were the most cynical in the beginning.

Why do I lay this out for you? I hope to help you with your questions and concerns. I would love to encourage you to see yourself growing and prospering while working for yourself. If you are a hard-working individual, and if you have big dreams, follow me through these stories of how people just like you went from doubt and skepticism to living the life of their dreams.

Chapter One

~

Network Marketing … The Perfect Business

"You don't have to be good to get started. But you have to get started to get good." ~ Jerry Clark

I f you are like hundreds of thousands of women and men worldwide who want to take charge of their lives, their finances, and their health, you might find network marketing to be a refreshing and viable alternative to traditional employment. Small business owners frequently discover distinct benefits in network marketing compared with other ways of working for themselves. Because the structure of this business potentially provides time and financial freedom to independent associates who take their businesses seriously, you may decide that network marketing is an excellent decision for you and your family.

WHAT IS NETWORK MARKETING?

First, it is also known as direct selling, multi-level marketing, relationship marketing, and word-of-mouth advertising. Products are sent directly from the manufacturer to the end user.

Distributors enable their customers to "buy direct" from the company.

The company relies on independent associates to let others know about its products. It is a "skip the middleman" concept; the sale happens person-to-person and occurs away from a fixed retail location. Associates typically do not carry inventory. In modern-day network marketing, the distributors enable their customers to "buy direct" from the company.

For more information about this industry go to Direct Sellers Association (DSA) at *http://www.dsa.org/aboutselling/* and The World Federation of Direct Sellers Associations at *www.wfdsa.org*.

People are drawn to network marketing for both financial and lifestyle benefits. Perhaps the greatest benefit is who you become along the way. Come for the money, stay for the friends you make and the person you become. Develop a new, heightened sense of yourself as a leader, an influencer, a master of your time, and a person of lasting significance. If you were not looking for these altruistic benefits, consider them a bonus.

Here is how you can tell if you are likely to succeed in this industry. Do you recognize yourself in this list?

- You seek alternatives to traditional employment. You are ready for a change.
- You are a "people person." You love to help others.
- You have a strong desire to do things beyond your reach with your current situation. For example, you want to live elsewhere, donate time or money to worthy causes, quit your job, or travel more.
- You are positive, entrepreneurial, and energetic.
- You are self-motivated and self-determined.
- You are able to focus on a project and stick with it until the results are in.
- You are turned on by learning and growing, and you embrace new ideas.
- You desire to be in control of your life, your finances, and your time.
- You have big dreams.

Factors to Consider When Choosing One Business Over Another

According to Tim Sales, network marketing legend, there are four factors to consider when choosing one business over another. They are:

- **Select a large and expanding market**. The wellness and direct sales industries are both booming. According to the DSA, there are more than fifty-eight million people involved in network marketing globally. The US-based National Bureau of Economic Research (NBER) and Recession Definition, Inc., report that health and wellness is the number one sector of the economy that thrives during a recession. Through good times and bad, the direct sales industry has grown *steadily* since the 1970s as other sectors and indicators have cycled up and down.

- **Choose consumable products**. When you market products that are consumable, your customers will use up what they buy. When your customers have grown to enjoy the benefits of these products, they will order more. Think of the difference between cars and shampoo. When your customers use the products they get from you on a frequent or even daily basis, you will receive ongoing orders that produce ongoing (residual) income.

- **Market products that are unique**. If your customers can get products like the ones you provide for half the cost at the local buyers club, the competition will wipe you out. If they rely on you for products that they cannot get somewhere else, you have a captive and loyal clientele. This enables you to create ongoing customer relationships.

- **Create a means to leverage yourself**. If you are going to work hard, why not get paid over and over for your efforts? In network marketing, you are not limited to your own efforts. You gain from the efforts of the entire organization,

When you are leveraged, you can accomplish more on a part-time basis.

as does every active, contributing member. If you will take the time and put in the effort to get your business up and running, you can eventually make money whether you are working or not—potentially a lot of money.

Can you open your mind to the concept of profiting from the efforts of a team, rather than working on your own? Do you have a vision of your life that is greater than what your job allows you? One of the many benefits of a network marketing business is that you do not have to stop what you are doing in order to succeed. When you are leveraged, you can accomplish more on a part-time basis.

According to research scientist Dr. Thomas Stanley, most millionaires became wealthy through business ownership rather than through traditional employment. He shares the results of this research in *The Millionaire Next Door*, *The Millionaire Mind*, and *Millionaire Women Next Door*. The information in these books cemented my decision to continue along the path of being a business owner instead of becoming an employee, working for someone else.

The Benefits of Starting Your Own Home-Based Business

For starters, the tax savings are tremendous. Many aspects of your life become legitimate, legal tax write-offs. What defines success is not how much you make but how much you keep. The average family can save thousands of dollars per year by having expenses they already incur become *bona-fide* business write-offs. That money can go toward savings, education, vacation, charity, and other worthy causes. According to Sandy Botkin, former IRS tax attorney, CPA, and founder of the Tax Reduction Institute, "The light at the end of the tunnel … is the financial opportunity that starting your own business offers. Every North-American taxpayer who works a full-time job and does not have a side business is probably overpaying taxes to the tune of $3,000 to $9,000 a year!"

A home-based business allows you to put your money to work for you in order to achieve time freedom. In this system you are leveraged financially, and your business can pay you every hour of every day and even when you are sleeping. What would happen if you did not have to go to work every day? If you have never made money in your sleep or while on vacation, or while you were playing with your kids, this benefit alone can be life-altering.

You can have a more balanced life. Working for wealth is different than working for wages. The control you gain enables you to make a whole new set of choices that are often unattainable when working for someone else. A home-based business supports family values. Not having to choose between family and work is a benefit for people with small children. One woman named Denise joined our team in order to be able to spend more time with her granddaughter.

Your income is residual. You do not have employees. You do not have to take from your earnings to pay employees. You do not have to carry inventory. Your start-up and operating costs are comparatively low, and your income is potentially high. You can work toward merely having your products paid for, or you can work toward rock-star income. You can make what you are willing to work toward by deciding how committed you are to acquiring the necessary skills to achieve the goals you have identified. There is no salary attached to your title and no ceiling on your income.

You can be mentored by people who know the ropes and who want to teach you to succeed. Often this hands-on training is at least as reliable—if not more so—as what you learn through more traditional educational systems. If you find a company with a vision and one that is in business to do dramatic work to make this world a better place, you may find that it is a privilege to work in this way. Many network marketers feel this about the companies they represent. We tend to be a pretty enthusiastic bunch because of the value we perceive in our work as well as the rewards we receive for doing it. Imagine working toward having your compensation be favorably disproportionate to your efforts. This equation is normally associated with heads of corporations who rake in staggering profits and bonuses. Now you know of a system where the average person can reap similar rewards for doing the most honest and honorable work of their lives. Might this be something you could see yourself doing?

Chapter Two

❧

The Entrepreneurial Gene

"Try not to become a person of success, but rather a person of value."
~ Albert Einstein

Robert Kiyosaki has built an empire through his books, seminars, CDs, and games about alternatives to traditional employment. His first book, *Rich Dad Poor Dad,* is a must read for anyone looking to become a business owner. The hypothesis that supports Kiyosaki's entrée into business coaching is that most people were brought up to consider the path of least resistance: get a good education, then a good job (with benefits), and retire with a pension. Kiyosaki has spent the last eleven years refuting the "wisdom" of that pathway as a way to financial freedom. He is quite emphatic about the benefits of being your own boss.

Current changes in the economy have forced many individuals to consider alternatives.

Rich Dad Poor Dad was first published in 1997. Kiyosaki was a forward thinker, given the changes in the job market since his book was written. In 2008 we witnessed the unraveling of job security at warp speed. Today, job and security can hardly be uttered in the same sentence with any semblance of veracity. Current changes in the economy have forced many individuals to consider alternatives, including options to which they might not have been open before. Recently, at a business seminar for approximately four hundred people, the speaker asked the members of the audience to raise their hands if they were certain their job would be there for them in one year. About eight hands went up.

This is relevant for those of us who believe that working for ourselves is the right choice. We self-employed types want to avoid the crash-and-burn effect that sometimes accompanies working a regular job. This discussion is not meant to disparage regular employment. Rather, it is designed to openly discuss the merits of business ownership for anyone who wants and needs to find a new way of working. If this is you, perhaps you want to know what it takes and if you can succeed.

Have you ever longed to be your own boss? This means waking up in the morning, seeing your face in the mirror, and knowing that you are the person for whom you are working. This concept is more challenging, perhaps, if you were not born with an entrepreneurial spoon in your mouth. For some, being our own boss is an obvious fit. For others, even with the job security rug pulled out from under them, it is still quite challenging to wrap their minds around not having a job to go to, not having to punch in, and not having a boss. But there is good news. In order to succeed, it is not necessary that you have always wanted to be your own boss. *It may be your experience working for someone else that provides the greatest impetus for you to succeed on your own.*

Both business ownership and traditional employment have their plusses and minuses. There are no guarantees along either path. If there is no entrepreneurial gene, what *does* it take to succeed as a business owner rather than as an employee? Let me tell you about someone I know named Judy who had decades of experience in the corporate world. What became the key to Judy's success was the contrast between her experience in high-tech management and the freedom and limitlessness of owning her own business. When she was making well into the six figures in her corporate job, she was not thinking of going into business for herself. When Judy got laid off during the umpteenth economic downturn, she had her wake-up call. She now owns and runs her own home-based business. The money comes in automatically every week and is residual. Her income now surpasses what she was making in high-tech. Judy says that she lost her job but got her life back.

What are the characteristics for success as an entrepreneur? See if any of these seem familiar to you.

- You crave more control over your time.
- You crave more control over your finances.
- You strongly dislike corporate politics.
- You have a very low tolerance for incompetence among your co-workers, peers, and your boss.
- You believe that you are restrained by your job and have a strong desire for autonomy.
- You know that a job someone gave you is also a job someone can take away, and this is completely unacceptable.
- You feel that you march to a different drummer compared with your co-workers.
- You dislike your job, not because you are lazy, unqualified, or incompetent, but because working for someone else may not be a good fit for you.
- You are unemployable because you find it is becoming more and more difficult to work for someone else.

Real security lies in being in control. If you can relate to this, and if you believe you can find others who think like you do, you may be quite good at network marketing. As you attract like-minded people, you may find yourself becoming more attuned with being a business owner. Would you like to fire your boss? Would you like to be more in control? Learn as much as you can about this business model. An informed decision to get involved may yield life-changing rewards for you and your family.

If there is an entrepreneurial gene, it is bequeathed by you to you through the unwavering pursuit of opportunities that lie outside of traditional employment. Turning your attention to these signs along the road will enable you to begin to pivot toward yourself as your own boss. As a business owner, you may work harder than at anything else you've ever done—professionally or personally. And if you are motivated and focused, and if you stay the course, you will be rewarded in ways that will eclipse all previous work experiences.

> If you are motivated and focused, and if you stay the course, you will be rewarded in ways that will eclipse all previous work experiences.

With the perspective of a business owner, you will discover that the great rewards occur over time, not overnight. At each step you become clearer on what you want your life to be and more determined about the results you are going to create. Becoming an entrepreneur has its challenges. But then the rewards are commensurate with the effort. Working for someone else has its challenges as well. We entrepreneurs believe that working for ourselves offers us more.

Owning your own business is about being in control. You are driving. You are steering. You are staring down your fears and blocks because you are clear and determined. Your dreams overshadow your fears. If you can believe in yourself enough to work until you succeed, you can say that you were born to do this. Once you gain clarity, nothing can stop you.

Chapter Three

∽

The Love of the Game

"I don't think I can play any other way but all out. I enjoy the game so much because I'm putting so much into it." ~ George Brett, inductee, Baseball Hall of Fame

B eing in business for yourself can be a pathway for allowing your creativity to flow. It is exciting to create something of value. Being in business for yourself means that your efforts come back to reward you and are not redirected to finance someone else's dream. Building is ongoing and a primary focus in business ownership. My dad's most recent business spanned over twenty years. He was building it up until the day he sold it at age eighty-five. I spent thirty years building and stabilizing my Rolfing and yoga teaching practice. Among other reasons, I knew it was time to move on when I no longer felt excited about building.

A friend of mine was employed at a high-tech company near where I live in the San Francisco Bay area. She scored a two-million-dollar account for her company. What did her company do for her? They paid her her regular salary. That was it. The return to the company for her landing that account represented inestimable profit. Even if that story is unusual or atypical, it still is amazing that people can work so hard and get such a little piece of the return for their effort. Of course there are stories of employees being rewarded enormously for contributions they made to the companies that employed them, but working as my friend does doesn't make sense to an entrepreneur.

Brian Tracy says that being the CEO of your life is required for personal mastery. This is the posture of a business owner. Robert Kiyosaki calls this "being on the right side of the desk." Positioning yourself to be the one to have the jobs to give to *others* is empowering. This is like stepping onto a playing field, determining the rules, picking which position you want to play, and choosing your teammates.

Remembering the benefits of working for yourself enables you to roll with the punches. After hearing about a business I was starting, one neighbor responded by saying with a note of horror, "Isn't that *risky?*" When I asked her to elaborate, she said that I must be crazy to do something that wasn't a sure thing. Hmmm ... being my own boss, making my own decisions, never having to get laid off, having a lot of fun growing and learning, and meeting amazing people. Brian Klemmer teaches that what we see really depends on what kind of lens we are looking through. My neighbor and I do not see through the same lens. As a matter of fact, she became chronically ill. She says it was because of all the stress at her job. I call *that* risky.

Entrepreneurs begin nearly every day eager to get to work. TGIM— Thank God It's Monday—is a twist on the beleaguered employee's familiar lament. What causes entrepreneurs to just about leap out of bed most mornings is the excitement they feel in the creative process. This process is a big part of the satisfaction that comes with business ownership and is valued as highly as the results. Many entrepreneurs love the journey as much as the destination.

> Many entrepreneurs love the journey as much as the destination.

Entrepreneurs work for a personal mission or vision. Sometimes we are so excited that we can't sleep, but this comes with the territory.

Going to work the next day means continuing to build a dream of a lifestyle and finding more people with whom to work. It is exciting in network marketing to know that there is limitless opportunity to build and profit. Some people absolutely love their jobs. But if the fire that burns in your belly is to be the creator of your own destiny, nothing is more satisfying than to build your dreams on your own terms. As Jim Rohn said, "It is easy to pay the price when the promise is clear."

It is difficult to understand how otherwise capable and smart adults tolerate being told how many hours they must work and how much vacation they can take. This remark may sound unpopular because millions of individuals live under this set of rules, decade after decade. If you are happy with regular employment, then you may find these comments unsavory. In fact, few people in that situation would pick up a book like this. But perhaps you are "on the edge" and are starting to tip toward being your own boss. If so, know that being in control of your life—especially in a business where you are taught to be free—is exciting, challenging, and potentially life-changing. It may not be for the meek of heart, but choosing to play will strengthen anyone's constitution.

It's not playing for "maybe" but playing for "yeah, baby!"

Fairly early into my network marketing business I was taught to play this game as if my life depended on it. But because I was new and did not know better, I thought that the people who were saying these things really should have gotten a life of their own. It seemed so *extreme* at first, a very narrow perspective. It was because I did not understand the value of freedom. Since I had not experienced it yet, I was not able to grasp this important message. As my organization began to develop I started to appreciate how wise these teachers were who came before me. I got serious about my business once I understood how life-changing the benefits of time and financial freedom were. The day I understood the stakes of playing as if my life depended on it was the day that my success was all but guaranteed. It is like the quote at the beginning of this chapter. Playing all-out ensures maximum satisfaction and the best results possible. It's not playing for "maybe" but playing for "yeah, baby!" If your dream is big enough, playing the game as if your life depended on it becomes the only way to go. You don't play to see what will happen. You play because you are going to make it happen. When you own your business, your efforts define the quality of your life. And that is the biggest game in town.

Chapter Four

❦

Treat Your Business like a Business

"If you're only willing to do what's easy, life will be hard. But if you're willing to do what's hard, life will be easy." ~ T. Harv Eker

Treat your business like a hobby, and it will cost you like a hobby. Treat your business like a business, and it will pay you like a business. These words are often the first thing a new distributor hears when launching her network marketing enterprise. This is Business Ownership 101.

The first rule of being in business for yourself is to go to work every day as if it were a job. If you have never owned your own business, approaching your workday like this will help you transition into being a profitable entrepreneur. The sooner you take your business seriously, the happier and more prosperous you will be in your new venture.

The second rule is to get in the game and stay in the game. Obviously you must take the first step by starting your business. And equally important, you must remain active over time in order to prosper and to develop yourself into a competent and seasoned professional.

MAKE A PLAN

Ideally, your sponsor will work with you to create a game plan so that you can lift your business off the ground as soon as possible. This plan is tiered in order of "achievability." It can vary from one individual to another, but it might look something like this:

- Get your products paid for.
- Recoup your initial investment.
- Earn additional income.
- Match, replace, and perhaps exceed your existing income.
- Achieve complete financial freedom.

The details of this plan will depend entirely on your goals, your level of ambition, how much time you are able and willing to allocate to your business, and whether or not your network marketing income is going to be your primary or secondary source of revenue. This should be discussed openly with your sponsor from the beginning. It can become an ongoing dialogue as you, your vision, and your business evolve.

I recently had the pleasure of interviewing Madeline, one of the top earners of a network marketing company, for a team training call. She had a treasure chest of wisdom to share. Madeline started her business fourteen years ago with the goal of getting her products paid for. At the time, she had four small children and only worked a few hours per week. Her customer base grew gradually as she shared the products with people she knew. She never became aggressive in her sales attempts. For years she never ventured outside of her circle of friends and acquaintances, enrolling a few friends and helping them enroll a few people whom they knew.

Madeline's efforts were building to something far more significant than her initial goal.

What Madeline realizes now, but did not see then, is that her efforts were building to something far more significant than her initial goal. If she had it all to do again, she said she would have been grateful for those few hours per week she was able to devote to her enterprise, instead of always telling herself that she was not doing enough. She did not foresee herself achieving her current status with her company and influencing as many people as she has over the years.

If you want to make ten thousand dollars per month within one year of starting your business, and you have only five hours per week during which you can work your business, you will need to adjust either your goal or your activities. Ideally your sponsor will help you figure out how much time and effort is necessary for you to achieve your goals and what you can realistically expect from the time you *can* allocate to your business. Discussing your goals with your sponsor will help you steer through this initial start-up phase. With an understanding and appreciation of the fact that you will need to put time into your business before you see significant results, you will be better prepared to defer gratification as you give your business time to stabilize.

If you are enrolled by someone who is not treating *her* business like a business, you are encouraged to seek out someone else in your leadership line who can help you. Talk to the person who enrolled *your* sponsor; work your way up the line with phone calls and e-mails. If you cannot find anyone, call your company to get names of other leaders in your area. If you are with a company that provides its associates with excellent training resources, and if you are determined, you should be able to succeed on your own. Some top earners were "orphaned" by their sponsors, which means that their sponsors either quit the business or were unwilling or unable to provide training and support. If you really want to make it in this business, please do not let the fact that your sponsor is unreliable or unavailable stop you.

PEOPLE WHO NEED PEOPLE

It is important that you start your names list shortly after you complete your application. This list is the basis for identifying people with whom you might like to work and who might be interested in your products. No names list, no business. Your names list is as important a tool for you as a hammer is to a carpenter

Who will you contact, and how will you find people? Some distributors prefer to do all of their marketing online, with leads, virtual ad campaigns, and social media. However, keep in mind that most people get introduced to this business by someone they already know, or someone they meet personally. Even if you meet someone in a chat room or from an Internet lead, you must focus on establishing a relationship with that person. You need to develop your ability to deepen your connections and build rapport with the people who are considering your business and your products. You must connect with people before either party decides to work with the other.

Since nobody with whom you speak *must* become your next associate or your next customer, you can relax. If you think that someone could be the next superstar in your organization, keep your expectations in check. The only person who has the potential of being a big contributor and strong leader on your team is someone who is willing to make building his business a priority and take this seriously. Discuss goals openly with all of your prospective business partners. Separate your needs from these conversations with people, and you will exert less pressure and feel more at ease. You will also be better prepared to

Make it about the other person.

listen to what someone wants to achieve if you suspend what *you* want during the discussion. The mantra is: *Make it about the other person.* Serve more people if you want to sell more products and enroll more associates into your organization.

RESOLVING YOUR CONCERNS

If you are unsure about network marketing, it will be difficult to encourage others to believe in what you are doing. If you have not experienced your company's products, it is unlikely you will market them successfully. Educate yourself about your company and the industry so you can speak reliably about both. Become your own best customer and product user. You want to stand tall and firm in your secure knowledge of the value of what you are offering.

In order to feel steady as you begin to build, you'll need to develop five primary areas of belief:

- Your company
- Your company's products
- The industry of network marketing
- Your company's compensation plan
- Your ability to succeed in this business

Your unshakable belief is what you relay when you speak with people. We call this your "posture." It is a combination of what you say, how you say it, and how self-assuredly you communicate with others. It has to do with standing tall as you talk with people about your business and your products. If you practice communicating with confidence, especially when someone challenges what you do and your beliefs about it, you too will develop good posture. The stronger your belief, the more people you will influence. When your belief is strong, no matter what anyone says, you will not get knocked to the ground and your journey will be much smoother. If you encounter "dream stealers"—people who want to talk you out of your new business and the goals you have set for yourself—you remain steady and confident.

Gradually, the final and most important belief kicks in: belief in you. It cannot happen overnight, so try to stay grounded and focused as you build up this cornerstone of your business. You may have been blessed with high achievement and expertise in another field, perhaps the one you were involved in when you started your network marketing business. Even if you have already done well elsewhere in your life, it is your belief in your ability in *this*, your networking business, that is essential for you to build a thriving and sustaining organization Believing in yourself and feeling confident in your new venture may come in fits and starts, but come it will as long as you are continuously practicing and improving

I encourage my team to go out and make as many mistakes as are necessary on their road to becoming competent. There is simply no better way to learn and improve. I get excited when someone on my team calls me to tell me how badly a follow-up conversation went. I praise her for bringing me something to work with as we begin to examine where things might have gone wrong, and how she can improve the next time. It is from these experiences and so-called mistakes that growth occurs. I have yet to meet a top earner in network marketing who does not feel that she made countless errors early in her career. Keep the faith, even when you think you messed up. Put yourself out there, swinging the bat and being willing not to be perfect as you grow and improve.

Filling Your Funnel

Your funnel represents the people who are in various stages of reviewing material about your products and your business opportunity. Your business will grow as a result of your finding loyal product users as customers and good, strong, motivated individuals for your group. You will be solely responsible for this by keeping yourself in production mode and continuing to contact people as you develop your network. Just as a dentist needs teeth to repair, you need people to be looking at your products and your business. The more prospects in your funnel and the more skillful you become at helping them understand the benefits to them of your business and product line, the more likely you will develop a strong customer base and a thriving organization of active distributors.

Successful entrepreneurs develop simple, effective routines that they repeat day in and day out over a long enough period of time to eventually experience quantum returns. For example, Jacqueline is a realtor who was very busy when she started in network marketing. In the beginning, she built her networking business by looking for just a couple of strong team members to help launch her organization. She decided to build her business by doing two things every week:

1. She made calls every Wednesday morning from nine to eleven-thirty.
2. She attended one opportunity meeting with at least one guest every Thursday evening.

She did not experience immediate results, but because Jacqueline was persistent and consistent, after a couple months of this activity she brought two very strong members into her organization. Both immediately focused on building *their* organizations. In this same time period, Jacqueline also picked up two loyal customers. The return on both of these placements is potentially quite significant. The results did not develop overnight, but they could pay Jacqueline back indefinitely.

Follow-up is the key. You must discipline yourself and develop the skills to effectively reconnect with people who are somewhere in the process of evaluating what you have to offer them. This habit should be incorporated into your daily routine. As you fill your funnel, keep track of people who are not interested now but who might be more open-minded later when their circumstances change. Keep notes on these people so you can help them move forward when they are ready to take action. You will need some kind of system to remember all of the people with whom you have spoken and where you left off with each person. What material have you shared with this person? What were his concerns? When did you agree to contact him again? Whether it is an old metal box with file cards or a completely high-tech electronic contact manager, the only thing that matters is that you put your system to use consistently.

Get into the habit of paying attention to what people say in order to find a legitimate way to start a conversation. Notice people in stores who have good customer service skills. Listen for people who say something about a desire to make a change in their lives. Notice the people in any club or organization where you belong who stand out in the crowd. Observe the trainers at your gym who are good with their clients. Keep your eyes and ears open for people who want more money, more balance, more time with their families, better health—whatever is going on for them. Look for people who seem to interact well with others. The friendliest teller at the bank is someone with whom you might like to chat. The purpose is to make connections.

> Listen for people who say something about a desire to make a change in their life.

The Approach

Learning how to effectively approach people to see if they might be interested in your business and products is among the most important skills you will acquire. In the early days of your business you will need to talk with many more people relative to the number who will actually want to buy your products or join your organization. This is an important time to keep your expectations in check. It is also the time that you are climbing up the learning curve, honing your expertise. Checking in with your sponsor, role-playing, and using all of the training tools that will be made available to you will make a world of difference. As you get some success under your belt, this aspect of network marketing can become a lot more fun and less daunting than in the beginning. I have found after considerable practice that I have been able to attract loyal customers and strong business partners with much greater ease with each passing year. Now, after many years in network marketing, it seems that I attract quality customers and new associates everywhere I go. This was definitely not my experience in the beginning.

If you or the person you are enrolling has concerns about approaching friends and family, take heed. The very nature of network marketing is word-of-mouth advertising. You should learn how to approach friends and family in an ethical and professional manner. Learning approaching methods that honor the relationships you have with people you know, you love, with whom you work, and about whom you care will be very good for business and ultimately good for the people who you approach. If you chose products that you believe can be of great benefit to those who use them, it should become apparent to you that it is your job to be the spokesperson for your company so that others can learn about them. Why would you want to deny the people about whom you care most the benefit of the products that you now distribute? Only fear and a lack of know-how could get in your way. Resolve both by learning the ropes. Your warm market—people you already know—is a gold mine for getting your business off the ground. And with the proper mind-set, you are offering your friends and family a gift by sharing with them the benefits of your products and, for some of them, your home-based business opportunity.

As you begin your approaches, always remember what the late, great Jim Rohn said: "Don't wish that it were easier. Wish that you were better."

Here are some tips for successfully approaching someone about your business and products.

- Do not say anything about your products or about the opportunity until you know that the person with whom you are speaking has a need or want that you believe you can help him achieve.
- Think of yourself as a purveyor of information and a resource for solutions. Be a trustworthy advisor, always keeping the other person's best interest in mind.
- Be disarming by telling someone that you do not know if she will be interested. By letting her off the hook, she can relax more and hopefully listen better.

- Create conversations with people. Communicate; do not lecture. Ask questions to engage people in the discussion. One of the most common mistakes made by someone whose communication skills are lacking is to ask a question and then neglect to give the other person time to think of his answer. Conversely, a good communicator asks questions and waits while the other person takes the time to consider the question. "John, you are nodding your head in agreement. What does this information about living a longer, healthier life mean to you?" Pause. Give John a moment to reflect.

- Once the dialogue begins, I let people know that as a result of their listening to the information I have to share with them one of several things could happen: they might become interested in my products and in becoming a customer; they might be interested to learn how to do what I do, which is recommend the products to others for profit; they might be interested in neither at this time; or perhaps they would consider referring someone they know to me. Any of those outcomes is fine with me; I will help them see if there is anything of benefit for *them* in what I offer.

- When speaking with prospective associates or customers, you might wonder whether you should lead with the business or lead with the products. Instead, listen to what they need and *lead with your heart.* Listening to someone's interests and concerns will guide you in knowing best how to serve her with your products and/or your business opportunity.

When approaching someone, here are two techniques to begin a conversation. I call this the "I Thought of You" method.

- I thought of you because … [Fill in something that this person wants or needs that you believe can be addressed by your products or business.]

    a. I thought of you because you have recently talked about wanting to lose weight.

    b. I thought of you because you have mentioned lately how tired you are at the end of the day.

    c. I thought of you because you told me last week that you are unsure about the security of your job.

    d. I thought of you because you told me you did not know how you would balance having a new baby with working.

    e. I thought of you because as long as I have known you, you have been talking about wanting to be your own boss.

- I thought of you because … [Fill in something about this person that represents a skill or talent you see as a potential asset for your marketing organization.]

    a. I thought of you because you are one of the most outgoing people I know.

    b. I thought of you because you seem driven like I am, and I like that about you.

    c. I thought of you because I see what great leadership skills you have.

    d. I thought of you because you are a walking billboard for healthy living and taking great care of yourself. (You can adjust this to reflect the products or services your business offers.)

    e. I thought of you because you have excellent people skills.

    f. I thought of you because you are one of the most goal-oriented people I know.

    g. I thought of you because of your passion for serving others.

The first rule in using the above techniques is that you must speak the truth. Do not cheapen any of these conversation starters by being insincere. Even if you are using the most sophisticated online tools, ultimately people will join your organization because of *you*. The videos, Web sites, CDs, DVDs, and testimonials you share

> The videos, websites, CDs, and DVDs are the *tools*. Building relationships based on authenticity, service, and trust is the *craft*.

with your prospects are the *tools*. Building relationships based on authenticity, service, and trust is the *craft*.

THE INVITATION

Once you have begun the conversation with a prospective associate or customer, you will want her to do something to learn more. That could be any of the following:

- Sample some products
- Watch a DVD
- Visit a web site
- Read a newspaper
- Attend an event
- Attend a webinar
- Meet with you
- Listen to a full presentation

You will find that people will not always follow through on their promises to try products, review materials, or even show up for events. Succeeding in this business requires a lot of patience. I don't stress when someone reschedules an appointment or does not do what she said she would do; nor should you. But once someone is engaged, I monitor her diligently, for it is my responsibility to help her move forward. My job is to help someone do something that is in her best interest. If things do not go as I had hoped, I must remind myself that some of the greatest connections I will ever make—in life and in business—may be the result of a slow start. You can begin with the end in mind, which is to help people see the personal and specific benefits of using your products and joining your organization. But do not let yourself be blinded by that vision. Create interest and reduce resistance. Taking things step by step increases the chances that you will stay connected to and be in harmony with people.

While your prospective associate or customer has materials to review, it is good to touch base, ask him if he has any questions, and say something genuinely encouraging that is personal to him. For example, for the man who recently joined my organization, I focused on the fact that he is a fitness trainer and is in incredible shape. I mentioned that I was excited to find out if he saw how he might incorporate the weight management products my company markets into his work with his fitness clients. Use word pictures to paint a mental image of how the person with whom you are speaking may benefit from what you have to offer. When I enrolled a public school teacher, I asked her if she was open to having an event to which we would invite other teachers who, like her, wanted to earn more money. I also told her that I was excited to put her teaching skills to work, since much of this business entails training others. Use your imagination to help people see how they can work within their communities and within their own circles of influence to help expand the network. You must help people visualize themselves being successful.

> A new associate who repeatedly tries to convert people who have no interest in a business like this might actually quit because working against people is incredibly unpleasant.

The sequence is fairly predictable, although variations will present themselves. For example, what begins as a discussion about the business might evolve into a conversation in which someone decides to be a customer. The opposite can happen as well. The key is to be flexible and to listen to what the other person wants and—just as importantly—what she says she is willing to do. If someone tells you that she would never, ever consider taking nutritional products—or whatever your product happens to be—that she doesn't believe in them, and that she has no interest whatsoever in learning about the benefits, you can try to convert her, but I do not recommend this. In a situation like this, there is probably too much resistance. A new associate who repeatedly tries to convert people in this way might actually quit the business because working against people who are very close-minded is incredibly unpleasant.

PRESENTING

The most successful business leaders learn how to give an excellent presentation of their company's products and business. The best network marketing companies provide their distributors with standard presentations in a number of formats that highlight the company's business and products. Top distributors may also share presentations that they themselves develop or modify. Whether you're a new associate or you have been in the business for a while and now want to move to the next level, the smartest way to acquire and hone your presentation skills is to continually tune into presentations provided by your company and its top distributors. If possible, acquire a recording of one of these excellent presentations and have it transcribed. This will be an invaluable basis for your own presentation. It may take you a few months to become proficient at giving a top-notch presentation, and you will definitely have to practice quite a few times. But doing so will reward you for the rest of your networking career.

Working with a variety of personality types has taught me the importance of being adaptive while building personal connections with prospective customers and associates. If you are super-high-energy or have an aggressive personality, you may need to tone it down just a tad to make sure that you are not overwhelming the person with whom you are speaking. If you tend toward introversion and are very soft spoken or even shy, you should become more animated and perhaps more assertive when giving a presentation. In either case, learning how to move toward the middle is good practice for learning to be a more expressive, well-rounded person. Whatever you can do to enhance your ability to connect with another person will be good for your business and good for your own personal development. Top earners in network marketing continually practice their people skills, seeking to master the art of connecting with others. They also tend to be genuinely enthusiastic and excited about their products and business. This is something worth striving toward if you want to take your business to the next level.

As one who enrolls new associates on a consistent basis, I have studied and practiced numerous aspects of communication, persuasion, influence, listening, and selling. I realize that when I am sitting across from a prospective customer or associate, it is up to me to do a good job of relaying the possibilities that could alter the course of this person's life. Because it is my intention to help people improve their lives as well as to bring on as many qualified new team members as possible, I have a few personal mandates that shape every presentation I give. It is the *direct communication* of these core values that I believe supports my ability to consistently bring new people into my organization. You too can practice these.

- People will encounter hurdles as they consider the business. You can address these hurdles one at a time and discuss them openly as you move along in the discussion. For instance, one hurdle that people frequently encounter is that this is a home-based business. You should mention that although we interact with other people regularly, there is typically no office outside of the home where we conduct business. Find out what the other person thinks about this. With someone who is 100 percent positive that he wants a regular, nine-to-five job and that he has no interest in learning about alternatives, I have chosen—and recommend that you do in a similar case—to let this person know that network marketing is probably not a good fit. With people who seem interested and curious, discuss the benefits of your products openly and ask the prospect if she would tell others about them if she knew what to say and how to say it. We train our new associates. Is the person you are sitting across from trainable? It takes about ten hours a week to launch a business like this. Is that feasible? You should identify the hurdles relevant to *your* opportunity and discuss them frankly.

- Think continuously that you are helping the person with whom you are speaking understand the value of your company's products and business opportunity. Your job is to explain how the products work, how we make money, what the training entails, and what the lifestyle benefits are. When presenting, the more you help, the more your business will grow.

- Engage your prospect. A great presentation is more a conversation and less a lecture. Ask for feedback. Encourage questions and concerns. You want the other person to participate in moving this conversation forward. As part of your discussion, explore the benefits for the prospective associate. How many ways can you see eye-to-eye with this person with whom you are considering a working relationship? The mini-agreements that you create with the other person become the building blocks for forming a full-fledged business partnership.

- I recommend and adhere to a strict no-hyperbole rule. When you talk with someone, make sure she gets a sense that you are real and that the information you are sharing is level. Tell it like it is. In *Influencer*, the authors (Patterson,

Trustworthiness trumps exaggeration every time.

Grenny, Maxfield, McMillan, and Switzler) state that if we want to influence someone to do something, it is important to be trustworthy. Avoiding hype and manipulative alterations of the truth will enable you to be even more influential. Trustworthiness trumps exaggeration every time and is a key ingredient among members of a stable organization. The no-hype rule begins when you first speak with a prospect, and it continues well into the presentation and beyond.

- Have your prospect's best interest at heart. When your intentions are pure, you can help the person with whom you are speaking to be more open and receptive. Ask your prospect to consider you as an advisor. Let her know that you will be considering everything about her situation as you make recommendations.

STAYING IN THE CONVERSATION

If you want to put to rest any concerns you have about your prospective associate or customer's objections, ask for them. You can say this: "Jamie, along the way, hopefully, you will have questions and concerns. Let's make sure to get them out in the open, and I will address them as best I can." When you discuss her concerns with her in this way it helps her feel that you are there to help. If you hear an objection that you do not know how to address, tell her that you think it is a terrific question and that you would like to do some research or perhaps bring someone to the discussion who has more experience than you do.

You can guide a conversation toward higher ground with a positive attitude. Saying "I am so pleased how this conversation went today" conveys to the prospect that you are not attached to a different outcome, you accept his position, you appreciate his concerns, you don't need for him to make a decision today, and other subtle cues that keep him engaged. Recently, I spoke with a woman who apologized for not wanting to meet with me until she had seen the online Web tour. I told her that was an excellent decision and I looked forward to sending her the link. It doesn't matter if I wanted to meet with her in person if she was not ready or if that is not what she wanted. By having her decision validated, she feels good about the next step, and we can move forward together. In fact, during this particular conversation, she started off sounding skeptical and hesitant. By the end of the conversation, she thanked me and told me how much she was looking forward to reconnecting with me the next week.

TIME TO ENROLL

By the time you have gone over all of the material, you may have a new friend. The person who is sitting opposite from you has gotten a sense of you. She feels honored and supported. The encouragement you have offered along the way has been genuine and personal. You have addressed her questions openly and responsibly, and she knows that you have her best interest at heart.

I always let a prospective associate know that the outcome will be up to her. If she wants to move slowly, I will be a step ahead of her with fresh ideas to help her achieve the goals she sets for herself. If she wants to move very fast, I will be a step ahead of her to ensure that she gets exactly what she needs to move her business along quickly. I let her know what she can count on me for, and we talk about what is expected of her in terms of contributing to the organization. What special talents does she have from which the rest of the group can benefit? Teachers are encouraged to teach, fitness trainers are encouraged to present the benefits of the products to athletes, and corporate warriors are asked to shed light on organization development. I help people feel that they can make a difference to the entire group.

By the time you have gone over all of the material, you may have a new friend.

By now in the process, everything has been discussed, and an enrollment is the natural next step. The person who is right for this business will often self-enroll by asking you what is required to become an associate. A pattern has emerged in which *everything* has been talked about openly. Trust has been established, and you have moved together toward a partnership. A seasoned associate knows the difference between encouraging someone at the right time and pushing back against someone's resistance. The former feels good and will make you want to keep doing this business. It is a function of sensing when someone is ready for the next step and having your encouragement align with the person's eagerness. The latter causes both parties to feel uncomfortable and explains why some people want to quit so early on. Trying to get someone to do something against his will is very different from helping him get what he wants. When you sense that someone is excited and ready to join your organization, offering to help him become a member of your team is the natural progression.

When you help people feel good about starting their business with you, you increase the chances that they will want to continue to be in business with you and will want others to join *them*. A lasting partnership starts with you as the person whom others trust. You have been impeccable every step along the way, and you have earned your title as *leader*.

> A lasting partnership starts with you as the person whom others trust. You have been impeccable every step along the way and you have earned your title as *leader*.

You have not tried to force the wrong person into your business. You have focused all of your energy in working with people who participated with you, in moving the process forward. You didn't push against people. You were in the flow.

TRAINING AND DUPLICATION

Upon completing the application, every new associate will need to make time to learn the ropes. This should be a priority, particularly for those who are eager to enjoy the financial and lifestyle benefits attainable through network marketing. As the enrolling sponsor, you should teach others to use as many of the tools available from your company as possible. This ensures that you and the rest of your organization have access to the same material for learning and prospecting. It is incumbent upon all associates to have completely reviewed the training material themselves in order to responsibly pass the baton to new members of the team. In the beginning, a new associate should avoid trying to reinvent the wheel. Mastering the basics as taught by the company through its training program serves the new associate, the entire organization, and all of the people with whom the new associate is speaking. If your company does not provide training material, you will need to be proactive in devising a system for you and your future business associates.

I divide my time between helping new partners get trained and talking with others who are looking at the business and the products for themselves. If you are in a position to help someone new become secure in her new business, know that this is an incredible use of your time. Imagine that the person with whom you are working could become an asset to your organization forever. When everyone has declared their own dreams and goals, these training sessions become a time for everyone to help *others* in achieving them.

Strong leaders in network marketing emphasize in their training the value of teamwork. In my organization, existing members welcome new team members via e-mail right away. I always introduce new members to people who are in the same branch of my organization as well as to other leaders on the team. When someone new feels connected to and supported by others who have more experience, this social bonding will increase the chances that the new associate will remain committed. As a team leader, you should encourage these relationships on a continuous basis. Some of the greatest contributors in my organization have made friends with people whom they did not necessarily enroll, or who were not enrolled by them. Invite others to encourage and offer support to new members in order to foster these bonds. When new associates discover that they are now connected to other like-minded entrepreneurs, they will take their businesses more seriously and be more inspired to treat their business like a business. Each person who does this is a jewel in your crown and should be treated like the gem that she is.

Chapter Five

～

Cracking the Code

"Become a time management master." ~ Eric Lofholm

P erhaps all the hours in your day are already taken. And if you are
not quite *that* busy, at least the demands on your time seem very
real. Where are you going to find time to train for and build your new
business? You *will* have to take time out of your busy day in order to
build a thriving, stable, and profitable organization.

If you have never owned your own business, this might be
challenging. If you have a full-time job, you will need to build your
network marketing business during your off hours. One couple rose
to the top of their company's pay plan by presenting to prospects on
their lunch break. Since they had another business that was quite
time-consuming, this was the only time they could allocate to their
networking business. You will have to borrow time from other activities
that are on your calendar. Some people find that they can use the time
they previously spent watching television to make calls.

Jim Rohn talks about your day job as that which enables you to
make a living. If you have a job, this is where you get your pay check.
On the other hand, says Rohn, your network marketing business can

potentially make you a fortune. This is the difference between linear income and residual income. If you have a very strong desire for that ongoing income, you can make deliberate decisions about allocating your time because you see the value in building your business. In order to achieve this milestone, you may eventually need to borrow from the time spent in creating your linear income and invest it in building your freedom revenue. Some leaders have found success in gradually converting their jobs from full-time to part-time.

When I was approached about network marketing, I was seeing Rolfing and yoga clients as well as teaching classes six days per week. In order to make money, I had to be tethered to my practice. I told my friend and sponsor that I had no time to build a business. However, after about a year of only part-time effort I was inspired by the progress in my new venture. I stopped seeing clients on Mondays so I could focus exclusively on building my business. It was very scary at the time because I was totally dependent on my body-work income to pay the bills. After another year I started to see even more significant results, so I stopped seeing clients on Wednesdays. Next, Friday became a no-client day. Then, I dropped my classes on the weekends. All of this happened gradually. My business evolved and, along with it, so did my vision of what was possible. Things heated up when I treated my new business as seriously as I had my former practice, which I had run diligently for nearly thirty years. After about five years in network marketing I was able to stop seeing new clients, and I gradually dismantled my practice. Eventually, there were some weeks in my network marketing business in which I was able to make more money *not* working than I was in my previous career working to full capacity.

My story is different from what others have done who might have built faster or slower than I did. That is the beauty of this type of business.

> Eventually, there were some weeks when I was able to make more money not working than I was in my previous career working to full capacity.

Each person charts his own course, depending on his goals. According to Napoleon Hill, author of *Think and Grow Rich*, "A goal is a dream with a deadline." The force that influences what you do with your business is your own desire. I believe that someone who is highly motivated but extremely busy has a better chance at success in this business than someone who has all the time in the world but zero desire or need to improve his own life, increase his own income, or impact others' lives.

Whatever you do to make time for your new venture, do so with the realization of what brought you to this business in the first place. Shifting your schedule and your priorities can be for you what it was for me, a responsible and mindful course of action, even if it feels risky and scary. If you have a full-time job, working weekends and evenings on your network marketing enterprise makes sense when you understand that you are working to buy back your time and control over your day. Will this be challenging? Yes, of course. But when you make the connection that this investment of precious time is for the purpose of creating a life in which you are *more* in control of your time, it will be well worth the effort.

Consider your daily activities. Can you set office hours? Can you find time daily to do something to move your business forward? Can you put a sign on your door instructing your family not to disturb you for ninety minutes—or for whatever time you can squeeze out? Can you discuss your business goals openly with your loved ones and let them know the benefit to the entire family for their supporting you in your new venture? Some people make deals with their families. If you have to miss a family event because you want to attend a training session, you can promise everyone to make them their favorite meal the next night. Be a problem solver when it comes to finding time to work on your fortune income. Let your family know what you intend to create for *them*, and ask them all to support you.

This can be challenging for individuals whose spouses are not supportive. It's best to discuss your plan as openly as possible with your partner. If you are unable to enlist your significant other to be enthusiastic about your new venture, at least you should be able to come up with some agreements so your expectations are out in the open. You may be able to cut a deal that if you get a portion of each weekday to yourself to focus on your business, you promise to never work from Saturday night to Monday morning.

One man in our organization named Randy had a difficult time enlisting his wife's support. Because he really wanted the time freedom this business model could provide, he focused on what was in it for *her*. According to his wife, he was already away too much of the time. Randy promised her that if she could be flexible in the beginning, he would be more available to her and the family in just a couple of years. He pointed out to her that if he did not do this business, in a couple of years they would find themselves in the same time rut. Other individuals have offered to share the money they make. One man named Victor begrudged his wife's involvement in network marketing until her commission checks became greater than what he was making in his full-time job. This once-skeptical husband eventually became an active business partner.

> Sending someone product information via e-mail takes about as much time as making a cup of tea.

In practical terms, it helps to know that returning a phone call takes just a few minutes. Sending someone product information via e-mail takes about as much time as making a cup of tea. We call it "touch your business every day." Remember the woman who did not realize that her part-time effort would become something so grand? Give yourself credit for the small, daily actions. Remind yourself repeatedly that your small activities *will* add up, and that they will fuel your intentions, desires, and belief in what you are doing.

Understand the difference between being busy and being productive. Busy might look like this:

- Answering e-mail for two hours.
- Taking an hour to find a document you misplaced.

- Allowing someone to talk your ear off during a meeting with a prospect and not taking control of the time.
- Driving to a presentation that is an hour away, realizing that you forgot to confirm with the person, and discovering that the person is not there.
- Getting lost on Facebook without having anything to show for your time.
- Googling network marketing and reading about other companies and other distributors.
- Multi-tasking for an hour with the result that nothing was really taken to completion and you have only loose ends to show for your time.

Being productive looks like this:

- Reviewing information with someone genuinely interested in your products.
- Connecting with people and following up.
- Setting up three-way presentations between you, a prospective associate, and someone in your organization.
- Discussing your company's various enrollment packs with a prospective associate.
- Going over the training material with a new member of your team.
- Explaining to a new team member what tools you and others in the organization use for prospecting, and when and how to use them.
- Inviting guests to your next event.
- Going through your names list and contacting people to introduce them to your opportunity and products.
- Creating and offering incentives to encourage people to experience your products.
- Building and implementing a database for tracking prospective product users and team members.

- Forwarding via e-mail relevant new product information to someone whom you know would benefit from receiving it and offering a discount for his first order.
- Scheduling appointments to discuss your business and your products with prospective associates and customers.
- Getting referrals and following up with them.

Write down the most important things for you to do today and this week. Choose the ones that will cause you to stretch and/or that are attached to the most significant outcome. Typically your most productive efforts will focus on either business development or generating revenue. As an example, setting up a product demonstration at your local chamber of commerce can potentially produce new customers and associates for your organization. Get into the habit of doing the most important things first. Making this a habit can transform you as an entrepreneur. Use your planner to track daily and weekly activities. My master to-do list is always visible to me on my computer screen. I look at it daily and put a yellow highlight through the items as I complete them. This encourages me to continue to accomplish the big goals I have set for myself. Some of the extraordinary goals, such as achieving the next significant leadership level with my company, wink at me every day. By knocking out the items on this master list, I feel empowered to continue working toward the biggest goals I have identified for myself. I do not let them out of my sight.

EMBRACING SALES

I have read some books and listened to presentations by network marketing masters in which the authors insist that what we do in this industry is *share* rather than *sell*. Other leaders describe what we do as advising and consulting. I have found for myself that identifying with the highest principles

> Good sales people help others get what they want.

associated with selling and deciding to become an excellent salesperson has taken my business from good to great. Whatever you call the act of helping people select products or decide to get involved in a business, becoming proficient and skillful in this arena is required in order for you to achieve success in network marketing.

According to Eric Lofholm, master sales trainer, embracing sales and becoming good at it are the ticket for anyone to live the life she desires through service to others. Lofholm describes the sales process as one requiring integrity, compassion, and honesty. A good salesperson assists someone in moving toward and taking action designed to help the prospective client get what he wants.

It is useful for you to explore what associations you bring to the words "sales" and "selling." If your notions are antiquated and conjure up images of an arm-twisting, manipulative, deceptive, and sleazy used-car salesman, you can see why you might resist this aspect of your business. Perhaps it is time for you (or someone in your organization whom you are helping) to adjust your thinking. Being good at helping someone get what he wants and needs is a noble and worthy service and a profitable skill. Doctors do it when encouraging a patient to adopt healthy lifestyle habits. Teachers do it when helping a student improve her grades. And network marketers do it when we present the benefits of our products and our businesses to qualified customers and associates.

I was working with an associate named Molly recently who was struggling with her ability to sell. I encouraged her to think of the products her company offers. With whom would she want to share these products if she were not making a profit? Molly's face lit up. She was able to come up with five names without hesitation. Suddenly she understood how she was allowing her limiting belief to hold herself back. Molly loves to help people and quickly became excited to develop this side of herself through her network marketing business. This is the integrity to which Lofholm refers—having someone's best interest at heart. Being able to sell is cut from the same fabric as being able to serve. Both will help you develop personal power and inner strength.

If you can identify with this interpretation of selling and continue to attach positive values and attributes to it, you will find yourself not only becoming more successful and profitable, you will also benefit from having developed these talents that translate to increased self-worth and self-esteem.

SPEAK THE LANGUAGE

Listen to those who are successful in the business and practice saying what they say. Become fluent in all aspects of your business. When you work with your leadership line and listen in on what they say, you will become more fluent by association as well as by modeling after them. If you want to improve your Spanish, it makes sense that while on a vacation to Mexico you listen and speak as often as you can for practice. It is the same thing with your network marketing business. I hear from new associates all the time how surprised they are by the language they have acquired simply by listening to and practicing what they have learned from others. Get in the habit of speaking about various aspects of your business. If you wait until you are able to speak perfectly, you will never say a word. Take your mouth off mute.

My partners and colleagues tell me that when I give a presentation, it appears that I was born knowing how to speak fluently about my business opportunity, company, products, and pay plan. Nothing could be further from the truth. I practiced over and over and over again. I did it poorly, improved gradually, and am now called upon by my company to present on global webcasts. The formula is simple: practice makes improvement.

LIFE *WILL* GET IN THE WAY

You can expect that on a week in which you had envisioned making calls, the unexpected will happen. Family needs arise. Your dog gets sick. You receive a notice from the IRS that you are going to be audited. Your drier dies. There is a flood in the garage. The list goes on and on. It is best if you focus on what you *can* do and resist the urge to lament about those inevitable distractions. *In fact, the story you choose to tell about those distractions will attract others to join your ranks, rather than cause you to be derailed or disheartened.* Besides, in each of these circumstances you will meet people whom you otherwise would not have met.

Christina has two small children. She was ambitious and had fantasies of building her business quickly. Those fantasies collided with reality when her duties at her daughter's pre-school became a greater demand on her time. She could have groused about the distraction from achieving her business goals, but she is smart and saw this as an opportunity. Because she had more contact with other parents and teachers, she wisely decided to capitalize on these connections rather than view the situation as a drain on her business. She spoke to others how she was building her business in the nooks and crannies of her life. By remaining positive about how busy she was, Christina demonstrated to others who were interested in making more money how they might succeed even though they had responsibilities in *their* lives.

SIMPLE BUT NOT EASY

Learn the must-dos to build your business. You will need to use your company's products in order to promote them. You will need to share information about the product and the opportunity with other people. I like to call this part "turning people on to better health (or whatever your product is) and better finances." If you want to make a lot of money, you will need to invest time learning and studying. There will be costs for training, time required to attend local and corporate events, costs for marketing materials, and other ongoing outputs of your resources. However, when your network marketing business is run efficiently, you will find that the costs are a tiny fraction of what it costs to run a traditional business, especially relative to how much money can be made.

Recently I spoke with a couple who had been enrolled by an associate in my organization a few years ago. The enrolling sponsor told these people that they could make huge sums of money, that the enrolling associate would build their business for them, and that it would really help her out if they enrolled. Needless to say they have been floundering since they signed on. Our entire conversation focused on what was necessary to make something of their business. They re-enrolled themselves, this time with realistic expectations. They felt

> They realized that in falsely thinking that their business would be built for them, nothing would ever materialize.

better knowing the truth, that their success would require ongoing effort. They realized that in falsely thinking that their business would be built for them, nothing would ever materialize.

One of the gravest mistakes any associate can make is telling someone that the money comes easily and that the business will be built for him or her. This is no way to build a leadership organization. Why would anyone want someone on his or her team who is led falsely to believe that he or she won't have to work diligently over time to succeed? Do yourself, your prospects, and the entire industry of network marketing a favor: be real, be honest, and let people know that this business is simple—but not easy. People can make an informed decision when you have discussed frankly with them what kind of effort is required to achieve their lifestyle and financial goals. These people will become great assets to your organization when they have agreed to the steps you have spelled out for them during an honest and candid conversation. They can become partners for life.

The business of network marketing might be called network *listening*, or *connection* marketing. When you have made a firm decision that you are in this for the long haul, now your prospective partner—someone with whom you are speaking—is

> The business of network marketing should be called network *listening*, or *connection* marketing.

free to review material in a manner that works for him. If you were trained to use manipulative techniques that imply scarcity, you should bring yourself up to current industry standards and practices. Expecting others to take you seriously begins with your own attitudes and beliefs towards yourself and this work that you have chosen. When you treat your business like a business, your professionalism and commitment to serve others will encourage people for whom this business is a good fit to want to work with you and become part of your organization.

Chapter Six

∽

Your Story ...
Don't Leave Home Without It

"Don't say anything out loud about yourself that you don't want to be true." ~ Brian Tracy

One of the first things I learned early in my network marketing career was to have two compelling stories when I speak with people: one product-related story and one business-related story. I was fortunate in that I had a significant (and lasting) response to my company's products fairly quickly. My business story came about a year into the business when I had a major ski accident that required surgery and a long recuperation. My commission checks came every week while I was doing nothing in my business. It was these two events that caused me to appreciate what I had and to never look back. I learned how to tell this story earnestly and honestly in order to inspire others to take a serious look at the opportunity I had to offer for *their* benefit. What about my story represents potential gain to the person with whom I am speaking? Learning how to focus on the benefits to your prospects is one of the smartest things you can do, whether you are marketing your business full-time or part-time. Tell your story in order to persuade others. Take my advice: open your mouth, tell the truth, and come from your heart. The combination of your honesty, integrity, and sincerity is unbeatable. Add to that a genuine desire to help other people, and you are well on your way.

The other place where storytelling shows up is in the words you use to describe your intentions and dreams. Let's say that building a dream home is your greatest desire. Talking about this house is an important step toward the creation of it because you make it more real. Whatever it is—sailing around the world, perhaps, or adopting a child from another country—telling your story helps launch what you say you want. Whether or not that story becomes a reality depends on how committed you are and how much action you are willing to take. Telling the story about the dream home is important, but making that story come true must follow. In the same manner, telling the story about your plans for building a thriving networking enterprise is important. Believing in your story and getting others to believe in you and join you is your ticket to freedom.

It can be challenging to go from storytelling to life-living. It's this in-between phase where real change occurs. As you put forth the effort to take your dreams from story to reality, your life will be infinitely more satisfying, exciting, and meaningful. Your greatest accomplishments will require action, energy, effort, and focus on your part. This is why we say in network marketing that who you become is as valuable as how much money you make. It is important to understand that the telling of your story is a start, but it is not complete until you have tangible results.

Take your dreams from story to reality. Your life will be infinitely more satisfying, exciting, and meaningful.

Begin by talking about your dreams, goals, and desires. Often this story becomes the blueprint for a life of outstanding accomplishment. There is a poignant segment in the movie *The Secret* in which one of the presenters reveals how he told a story about his dream house in vivid detail. Years later he finds the picture of this house he had drawn in the past and discovers that he is now living in that house.

High achievers and successful people cannot tolerate a gaping hole between the story we tell and the life we live. The very purpose of the life of a high achiever is to close that gap. And then we find another story, and turn that one into reality as well. This is so remarkably satisfying that, for some people, the more they create, the more they create. It is as if a story is destined to come to life, like an animation that jumps off the page and starts to dance around the room. In the movie *Miss Potter*, Renee Zellweger's character, Beatrice Potter, draws characters who have a life of their own. These characters, like some of your dreams, cannot be contained in the imagination. They are destined to be brought to life.

Sometimes the mere telling of a positive story is where people get stuck. In network marketing, as in any business, there are the talkers and there are the doers. For example, a man named Paul spoke up at a seminar recently. He *said* he wants to become a top earner, but in fact he does nothing to contact people and invite them to look at his opportunity. This is something you want to be aware of. Your story can be a stepping-stone and empower you, or as it is for Paul, it can be a trap. The man who led the seminar was named Bruce. He had told a story for years about how he was going to sail around the world. What an exciting story ... until Bruce discovered that all he had was that story. Finally, he actually did sail around the world. Needless to say, making his story a reality was infinitely more satisfying than merely talking about it. This is not to disparage your telling incredibly positive stories about how you intend to live your life. High achievers do it all the time. Just make sure that you take action from there. Bruce said that not only was the experience of sailing incredible, but his entire life changed merely because he finally did what he said he was going to do.

HIGH ACHIEVER VERSUS SUPER STAR

In his insightful book *Mastery*, George Leonard cautions that the initial excitement of a new idea is not where the highest satisfaction is found. Once the buzz of something new wears off, it can seem as if you have flattened out. What, no instant results? There is a middle ground that must inevitably be negotiated. It is sometimes boring and tedious and un-fun, which is why many people get derailed. It is your ability to move from the start through this apparent plateau to becoming excellent at what you do that is the measure of your ability to create a life of meaning and purpose. This is where all of the satisfaction lies. It may be exciting to start something. But starting pales in comparison to actually completing what you started and becoming highly proficient. As fun as it is to dream, it is nothing compared to having your dreams come true.

In a network marketing organization, as in any professional group, there is a small percentage of people who zoom to the top. These people raise the bar for everyone else. Those in the top one or two percent make more things possible for the rest of the population, who may shift their thinking just by witnessing these super-high achievers. It is almost as if they defy the laws of nature, thus making the unreal seem more possible to those observing their astonishing feats. The twenty-four-year-old who flies to the top earning level in her company in record time leaves others breathless and amazed. For people like this, the impossible seems inevitable.

> As fun as it is to dream, it is nothing compared to having your dreams come true.

Superstars are the exception. They seem to break sound barriers with the speed of their accomplishments. But most people experience a big gap between themselves and the superstars. Do not let these heroic feats discourage you. There is good news for you if you are more the average type.

Jeff Olson addresses this pointedly in *The Slight Edge*. In essence, your ability to rise to the next level is relative only to what you have accomplished so far. By changing your actions to simple daily activities that support the growth of your business, you have written a new script and given yourself a new story to tell. If you are not where you want to be lifestyle-wise and with regard to your income, *figure out what the next step is for you and focus on accomplishing it.* You do not need to measure yourself against the superstars to produce amazing results in your life.

Typically in network marketing, growth is measured by the size of your organization, the size of your commission check, the improvements to your lifestyle, your company's leadership rank that you have achieved, and your ability to influence and lead others. You do not have to leap over tall buildings to create success for yourself. Just by becoming better, and continuing to hone your skills and abilities, you will have created your own slight edge. Extend yourself by taking simple daily actions consistently over time; this will put you in the winner's circle. If you want a larger organization, for example, and you have fallen back in your approaches, get to work in order to get results. By making it happen, you have rewritten your story and taken yourself to *your* next level.

If you don't like where you live, you don't have to move to a mansion to be happy. There is tremendous room between where you are and a palace. If you want a great relationship, you don't have to meet Mr. or Ms. Perfect to be content. If you want more money, you can achieve new heights without becoming a multi-millionaire overnight. What you want is attainable if you will put forth enough focus and effort over time to raise your own bar and start to craft a new and a different story. You can do this. If you are going to double your income this year, go tell *that* story and find others who want to come along with you. Commit to the action steps to make your story come true. Leaving your story in the realm of fiction puts you on the path that leads to nowhere. The more real you make your story by taking action, the more you believe in your ability to achieve better results. You can become a higher, more driven achiever, *relative to where you are in your life.* As you make this shift, the results you achieve will support and encourage you in continuing to move ahead.

An example of this in my life has to do with the caliber of associates I have been attracting to my organization and the ease with which I attract them. In years past I would have affirmed how hard it was to find good team members. That was my story. Telling it made it more real. Two years ago, I began to observe that more people were now coming to me to join the business. This was very different from my reality early on, which was that it was a lot of work to enroll a new associate. I turned my focus to this change and began describing this to others. The more I spoke about it, the more people came to me. The more people came to me, the more I told the story about this. There is a positive feedback loop when you attach yourself to what you want and lean into that with thoughts, feelings, words, and actions.

How do you show up?

Recently at a prospecting event, a woman named Myra was telling everyone about her new apartment. The mirror on the sliding glass door was broken, there was less closet space, and everything that can go wrong during the move did go wrong. The move and the subsequent encounters with the management of the apartment went badly. She was upset that the apartment manager had kept her waiting for over an hour to finalize the lease.

I asked her if there was anything about the new apartment that she really liked. Her face lit up. The view from the picture window overlooking the balcony was spectacular. The bathroom was at least twenty years newer than the one in her previous place. The kitchen was much more spacious.

Why hadn't she told us that first? Why did she go on and on about the bad stuff and withhold the parts that pleased her and that would have made her more enjoyable for others to listen to? Myra presented herself as a downtrodden, victimized complainer. I observed her standing alone at the event as people moved away from her.

Every time you open your mouth, you are relaying signals about yourself that will affect how others experience you. Paying attention to your words and your actions and *choosing* how you show up will dramatically improve how others will perceive you. You cannot cause others to have a certain reaction to you. But you can influence others by being mindful of what you say and what you do.

Here are some things to which you should pay attention:

- **How do you introduce yourself?** What do you say about yourself when others first meet you? Do you leak bad news to anyone who is listening? Do you recognize the other person with a smile and something genuinely positive to say?

- **How much do you listen versus how much do you say?** Do you go on and on about yourself, or do you focus on the other person? Are you busy being interesting, or can you focus on being interested? Hogging a conversation will not leave a positive impression on people. You already know about you. You should be more interested in learning about the person with whom you are speaking.

- **What is your emotional state when you interact with people?** Being able to contain whatever issues you are dealing with is good practice. First impressions make a difference. Just as some go to the gym to flex physical muscles, can you flex your emotional muscles when you meet someone? Managing your emotions is good for business. You owe it to yourself and the person with whom you are speaking to bring forth positive energy and to focus on things that will increase your "attractor factor."

- **What do you identify as the most important thing to discuss with others?** There are a million things to talk about when launching a conversation. Is this the right person to tell about running out of half-and-half for your morning coffee? Do you really want to pollute the space by telling a new person what a disappointment your brother has been to you? A good practice is to bring forth the brightest and most exciting things going on in your life as topics of conversation. This will be easier and more pleasant for the person with whom you are talking, and it will enable you to feel a lot better as well.

What you choose to talk about will affect your credibility with others. At a given moment, there are thousands of bits of data about your day, your life, your business. *What parts are true and positive?* What words can you string together that are honest and that will have the greatest impact on the other person's experience of you? Choose mindfully. Does it serve you to repeatedly promulgate the fact that some people find your products too expensive? That is a breach in your mindfulness and produces negative results when talking with someone who might otherwise be a good customer. Let's say you spoke with ten people this week who were not interested in your products and one person who was thrilled with the items she bought from you. The latter is exactly what you should be focusing on while conversing with someone.

> What words can you string together that are truthful and that will have the greatest impact on the other person's experience of you?

Some behaviors are best left excluded when you present yourself:

- Complaining
- Whining
- Blaming
- Making excuses
- Feigning victim
- Rudeness
- Self-absorption
- Gossiping

One associate in my group brought a man named Jack to my home for a product demonstration. Jack stood in my kitchen with his arms folded, swearing that he would not be able to succeed in network marketing. He justified why he was not the right person for this kind of business. He sure had a story and was shooting himself in the foot with it. How can you argue with someone who is *insisting* that he is going to fail?

Some people whom you meet may one day play a role in your becoming the person you are destined to become. When you open your mouth, you are sending a message about who you are and what you stand for. Your choices in what you say will determine what kind of people want to be with you. If you want to work with people whom you admire, be admirable. Become the positive person who attracts positive people as mentors and partners in your business. Drawing in the kinds of people who have the most value to bring to your life is a function of your accepting your own worthiness and knowing the value you bring to them. Let powerful people empower you as you become more powerful yourself. By continually working on yourself, you add value to who you are. Others will want to invest in you because of your increased self-worth.

The smartest thing you can do on your way to being a well-compensated entrepreneur is to get a little bit more accomplished every day. Never stop growing. Your business grows as you do. Continually step into the fresh, new, true story of your best life. Focusing on the positive and becoming more determined will help you stay on course. Push that envelope in order to create higher personal achievement. This will pave the way for you to start living your dream. And that is a story worth telling.

Chapter Seven

⌒

Say Yes

"If you can find a path with no obstacles, it probably doesn't lead anywhere." ~ Frank. A. Clark

The name of this chapter is inspired by a speech given by Collette Larsen at the end of a three-day international convention for associates of a network marketing company. Collette has been the top earner in her company for many years. Her message reverberated among those in attendance. Say yes means aligning yourself to live the grandest, most abundant, joyous life you possibly can. Say yes means giving in to your dreams, goals, and desires, and allowing them to manifest fully. Say yes means surrendering to a life that is about making a difference for others.

The promises made to prospective distributors have two faces. First, it is true that the sky is the limit with most compensation plans. With no ceiling on an associate's income, suddenly a whole new universe of possibilities presents itself. If you are a new associate, you will be encouraged to get clear on your desires during the enrollment process. If you are enrolling someone else, you should encourage the "newbie" to think bigger. Explore with him what is possible beyond his current situation. For many of us, our dream is one of the cornerstones of our decision to start and continue with this kind of business.

The other face of this promise entails the work you do on the inside. Put one foot in front of the other until you get what you came here for. Identify and challenge any limiting beliefs you encounter. Embrace opportunities for change and tackle any hurdles for the growth that doing so affords you. In order to produce something greater in your life, you will need to become a stronger and better person in the process. Become a master of your own inner game.

Although there is no simple formula, no "one-step-does-it-all" for you to achieve your dreams, there are mechanisms to help you live a more prosperous and fulfilling life. These three steps will help you begin.

1. Make peace with your desire to want more, to do more, and to have more. It is part of our human condition. Those desires are the impetus for your most significant contributions, creations, and personal satisfaction.
2. Develop a deep and lasting belief that you deserve to fulfill your desires. If you are willing to do the work, you are as deserving as anyone else.
3. Identify what it is that you want most. Your own categories may include:
    * Contributing to others (charities, sharing your resources in order to make a difference for others)
    * Material objects (where you live, what you drive, your wardrobe, your art collection)
    * Lifestyle opportunities (travel, time, freedom, being with family)
    * Personal development (education, developing leadership skills, becoming more influential)

It is so important to get clear on what you want so that you know when saying yes has the most value for you. Recently I was in Monaco, where I saw magnificent private yachts in the harbor. Although they were gorgeous, I personally do not want to own a yacht. However, when I see a picture of the countryside in New Zealand, a place I have not yet visited, I must say yes to *that* image because it matches my desire. Until you take the time to map out what *you* long for, there is no distinguishing among the continual array of gifts, possibilities, and opportunities you encounter.

This journey called life is a lot more pleasant when you surrender to your desires rather than resist them. I have lived in foreign countries before, and I would like to do that again. When my fiancé and I discuss in which country we would like to live for a year, we not only say yes to the possibility, but we breathe life into it by talking about it openly. Practice relaxing into the thoughts and feelings that accompany your desire. Let's say, for example, that you know in your heart that you would like to be a bigger contributor to a particular cause or charity. Sharing your resources with those less fortunate than you might be your hot button—the thing you want the most. This is where you might want to put your energy and your money. Think "yes" in your mind. See yourself contributing. Give what you can (even if it is less than what you want to give or think you should give) and give thanks for being able to do that.

> Get clear on what you desire so that you know when saying yes has the most value for you.

Some desires may be more material. This includes the kind of car you want to drive, your wardrobe, upgrading or changing your home, devices around your house and office to make life easier and more enjoyable, and and so on. Allow yourself to recognize anything you long for in these categories. On the other hand, what if your dreams are more about being able to do for others? If you learn about a trip to a foreign country to visit orphanages, and you feel a strong desire to do that, lassoing that desire and saying yes to it brings you a step closer to being able to do that yourself. You have an internal monitoring device that helps you attune yourself to those things for which you personally long. When you experience such a longing, get in the habit of saying yes to it.

Perhaps your dream is to go back to school, or to start or complete a course for which you have longed. You must honor and cherish this desire in order to help it come to fruition. Relaxing into the images and feelings that come with your having completed this desire is the underpinning of your saying yes. Saying yes is the opposite of resisting your desires. If you have habitually squelched them, this would be a good time to revisit them. There are mechanisms to saying no; it is useful to see if you are unwittingly implementing them.

Saying yes is the opposite of resisting your desire.

- Telling yourself that you do not deserve something.
- Falsely assuming that other people can have, do, or be someone or something, but not you.
- Dwelling on thoughts about why you are not meant to be the one to have a certain prize.
- Telling yourself it does not matter.

Your desires *do* matter; it is the progressive fulfillment of them that adds so much value to your life.

Just as you can turn on the mechanism that orients you to saying yes to what you want, you can turn off those mechanisms that have you habitually saying no. Both come with practice. Let's say you have always wanted to go on a cruise. Every time you see, hear, read, or think any cruise-related data, focus on anything positive about the cruise you can possibly imagine. Close your eyes. Whatever it is about the cruise that you want, imagine it fully and repeatedly.

TUNING IN

Thoughts have vibrations. They are accompanied by emotions and feelings in your body. Feeling joyous is accompanied by different thoughts and body sensations than feeling sad. Your body and your mind give you contrasting signals when you are optimistic than when you are depressed. Beliefs are thoughts you have reinforced enough times that you now perceive them as true. Being mindful of the thoughts and beliefs that cross your mind like an ever-present ticker tape is critical for you to make positive and substantial change. Becoming a top earner in network marketing, for example, is best accompanied by consistent thoughts and emotions that support this change in you. Planning for your success—mentally and emotionally—helps ensure it.

You must listen to the deepest layers where thoughts are formed inside of you. A thought may be the size of a pinhead, but it carries tremendous weight in terms of its influence on what you are able to create. As you quiet any disabling thoughts and turn your attention to ones of expansion and abundance, you will experience physical evidence of this new reality around you. Paying attention to every ounce of proof of abundance and affluence that appears in your life enables you to say yes to this reality.

I met Andrea at a networking breakfast. She had recently completed a work-related task for which she was given a substantial commission. I complimented her on her accomplishment. Although she is a highly capable individual, she was determined to declare herself poor and told me that she was undeserving of any praise. She insisted that although she made money this time, there would probably not be more forthcoming. She was arguing for more of what she does *not* want, which is "not enough money." Her thoughts and beliefs are the culprits that block her from creating the financial reality she desires. Even when money appears,

> One of the goals of personal development is to feel more peace and happiness and to be a more positive person.

she is saying no to it. Ask yourself if you have similar thoughts that run counter to your heart's desire. It is more difficult to create something when you are saying no to it because of this resistance.

One of the goals of personal development is to feel more peace and happiness and to be a more positive person. Through activities, such as meditation, stretching, exercise, and taking in proper nutrition you can learn to feel better and relax more effectively. Feeling good can be your default setting. The more you do things on purpose that produce these good feelings, the more you set your emotional thermostat to register at this place. If you know that eating too much junk food makes you feel lethargic and sleepy, notice it in order to help you make better choices next time. When you stretch or go for a walk, and as a result you have more energy and less tension, acknowledge it. You are teaching yourself to feel good on purpose. Feeling good becomes your new habit.

With no disruptions, distractions, or obstacles, your natural state can be one of joy. *You definitely want to identify this state of happiness and peace so that you can find your way back to it as often as possible.* You do this by continually paying attention to your body, your thoughts, and your emotions. With practice you will discover that how you feel is definitely impacted by what you think. Do you want to feel better? Notice and weed out the negative thoughts and begin replacing them with positive, life-affirming ones. As singer and song-writer Willie Nelson once said, "Once you replace negative thoughts with positive ones, you'll start having positive results."

Let's say you are driving your car and suddenly on the news you hear something about sagging housing values in your county. These are the types of triggers that might inadvertently trip you up if you are not paying attention. *You can tell if you reacted to hearing this by how you feel and the thoughts you think.* If you suddenly feel bad (tense, depressed, scared, worried, angry, or anxious) and if you hear thoughts firing off in your head like machine guns, you can know for sure that you reacted to this information. Try to remember that your natural state is happiness and peace. If you find yourself feeling down, you can always trace back to something that happened to which you reacted negatively. With practice, you will identify these triggers faster and spend far less time feeling off-kilter and not knowing why.

Pay attention to what you make up in your head. Your thoughts often seem to have a mind of their own. You may be responding to events in your environment, or the thoughts may also be triggered from the inside. If your mind offers up a thought that you react to, that you *focus* on, you can create a landslide of thought-based reactions, physical sensations, and cascading emotions all by yourself. Discipline yourself to pivot to other thoughts instead of reacting to your mind uncontrollably. Just as you might go to the gym to strengthen your body, you can use these practices to tone your mind.

You have a wide range of responses to learning that home sales have dropped in your area. Any knee-jerk reaction is best patrolled by the part of you that pays attention to your body and your mind. Don't just react. You can discipline yourself to remain centered and non-reactive. You can teach yourself to go upstream to a positive thought that can be as simple as, "Well, what goes down must come up." Or, "Wow, I am blessed to have a house!" Practice making up thoughts that are associated with appreciation, joy, and optimism. Now, instead of your mind controlling you, you are controlling your mind. There is literally a flow of thoughts and feelings inside you; with practice, you can determine in which direction they are flowing.

Listen to any old refrains in your head that are not in alignment with what you say you want. These are thoughts that ought to be corralled and sent to the place where old thoughts like this are retired. Begin to think new ones. Say yes to what you want, how much money you desire, where you want to live and vacation, how you want to contribute to your family and friends, and anything else that is on your wish list. Replace thoughts of worry and fear with one of the most empowering of all questions: *What do I want to create?*

Replace thoughts of worry and fear with one of the most empowering of all questions: *What do I want to create?*

Answering this question will lead you to a new and positive focal point. You are now being creative rather than reactive.

When your creativity is in full bloom, getting a job done and achieving your goals is easier and more enjoyable. You have lightened your load and created momentum within your creative self. The most difficult tasks are less daunting. For example, if you want to find leaders for your network marketing organization, consistently filling yourself with optimistic thoughts and positive beliefs about your own worthiness will fuel your achievement. Say good-bye to the resistance that took the form of self-doubt and negative thinking and say yes to what you want. As you manifest your vision, bring mind and body into alignment and say yes with your entire being.

Chapter Eight

⌒

Your Dream ...
Too Big Is Just the Right Size

"A dream that you can accomplish all by yourself is too small of a dream." ~ John Maxwell

I n *The Magic of Thinking Big*, David Schwartz suggests that the size of your dream is more important to your success than the size of your intellect. Getting out of bed to earn a paycheck is the reality of some who are employed in a regular job. But you must have a dream to go to work for yourself. Network marketing is more than a career track. It is about what you want to do with your life, which is why having a clear dream is such an important element.

I left a satisfying career in Rolfing and yoga to build my network marketing organization. It was a careful decision and one that I have never regretted. My sponsor encouraged me to pursue my dream in a way that no one ever had before. In my previous career, we often talked about professional goals. *But there was never a discussion on how the work we did made a difference in the lives we lived outside of work.* In network marketing, we are enthusiastic about our dreams. Organizations grow in direct proportion to the size and clarity of the vision held by individuals and by the team. This aspect of the network marketing culture was part of what attracted me the most.

Knowing what your very best life looks like and being willing to work toward creating that is high-level personal achievement. It is a grave mistake for any of us to think that we can skip over the dream-building part of starting our own business. In fact, getting over any resistance to hammering out your dream may represent an opportunity that supports both your success in business as well as a personal milestone. Last week I spoke with someone named Nancy, a very ambitious young woman (not in network marketing) who had her career path all mapped out. She was going to be vice-president of her organization, she was going to complete her degree, and she was going to take over her boss's job in five years. She was on fire. I asked her what she wanted to do with her life outside of work. Nancy gave me a blank look. She had no clue. *Her goals were limited to her work-related track and were not connected to her quality of life.* In network marketing, we work to create a balance between working and not working. It is important to know what we want to do with that time and that freedom.

> Knowing what your very best life looks like is high-level personal achievement.

Letting the universe help you get what you want is like sitting in a restaurant looking at the menu. When the waitress comes to your table and asks you what you want, if you do not know, what does she say? "I will come back later when you have decided." Likewise, the forces around you are ready to fall into step to help you get what *you* want. If you don't know what that is, you may have to wait a long time before your order is taken.

> In the beginning, my dreams were small and my problems were great. Very gradually the proportion of those two began to reverse.

You Have to Start Somewhere

In the beginning of my network marketing career, my dreams were small and my problems were great. Gradually the proportion of those two began to reverse. My dream is now crystal clear and has my attention the way my problems used to. There has been a complete shift of my focus. After countless hours of goal-related projects and training, I have it crystallized to four specific and equally important segments:

1. To leave a financial legacy for my children (they will inherit my passive income).
2. To help other people improve their health, their finances, and their lifestyles (coaching and mentoring people within and beyond my own organization).
3. To live a life of freedom with my life partner (traveling where we want, doing what we want, when we want, in the manner in which we want).
4. To travel the world, doing sports, on my own terms (biking, in-line skating, water skiing, downhill skiing).

If you tend to focus on your problems, you will be amazed how much happier and energetic you will be when you pivot to focusing on your dream. One of the mechanisms to facilitate this change is to find people who want *their* lives improved. The better you get at helping people get what they want, the more your own life improves. Remember that you have a viable business. By sticking with it over time, you can create a surplus of money, change the direction of your life, and bring others along with you.

If the restraints of time and money were lifted, what would you do differently in your life? Tim Sales, network marketing industry-wide giant, calls these "wants, needs, and don't wants." We network marketers eat this stuff for breakfast.

Pause for a moment and answer these questions.

- What do you want more of?
- What do you want less of?
- Why is this important?
- What will you sacrifice in order to achieve this?

Keep asking yourself questions like these. Eventually your dream starts winking back at you, beckoning you to put more energy into its manifestation. Allow your belief in your own worthiness and the fact that you deserve all of this to develop as you follow the training system given to you when you joined your networking organization. As you settle in to actually having this life of your dreams, another layer of belief washes over you. For example, if you have always wanted a weekly massage, perhaps you can start with getting one once per month. You are now closer to what you want, which prompts you to have faith, to keep building your business, and to find others to join you. When you know where you are going, and as you become more confident in your ability to lead others, you *will* find people to become part of your network. In what other industry can you experience this "dream fest?"

As you focus on helping others, your attention is diverted from your own problems.

Make your business be about helping others. Learn to listen and ask questions. As you start to get results—regular commission checks, new members to your group, a few loyal customers—you begin to relax, and your energy is freed up to focus on others. It may come in thimblefuls, but it does happen. As you focus on helping others, your attention is diverted from your own problems. Others are more attracted to you because of that shift. It works like pure magic.

You, Inc.

THE CARROT AND THE STICK

Different people are motivated by different things. Many times I have listened to what displeases people the most about their lives. Examples that come to mind include people not wanting to have to work a day job, not wanting to say no to their kids about family vacations, not wanting to drive an old car, not wanting to rely on a former spouse for child support, and not wanting to live in the same old apartment. In motivational terms, the stick represents what people are avoiding, like a donkey that moves forward because he does not want to get whacked. The stick represents people *moving away* from something. Avoiding pain is the first form of motivation.

The carrot, on the other hand, is the prize held out in front. The racehorse is moving toward the carrot as his reward. The carrot stands for *moving toward.* Examples of the carrot include more travel, being happier, feeling free, giving more to others, and being able to live a higher quality of life. This second form of motivation has to do with increasing pleasure: it feels good.

Although I was originally taught that these were simply two different motivational patterns, I have come to appreciate the wisdom of focusing on the carrot side of the equation. It is, however, important that you know what you no longer want in your life. Perhaps you no longer want a long commute, or you no longer want to run out of money at the end of the month, or perhaps you don't want a boss. *Once you get clear on what you do* not *want, turn your attention to what you* do *want.*

If you chant on and on how you want things *not* to be, you still have your attention on that. It is much more difficult for positive change to find you when your focus is on the negative. You can change these patterns by paying attention to your inner dialogue. Learning to meditate can help you quiet your mind.

If you figure out what you really want, and you help people get what *they* want, you will get back more than you bargained for.

76

Writing affirmations and repeating them throughout the day can also raise the vibrations of your thoughts. Be sure your affirmations are specific to what you want. Avoid affirming *not* having something, as in "I no longer have debt." When what you do not want (namely debt) is in the equation, you are still attached to whatever it is that you want to leave behind. "I have two thousand dollars or more left over every month after meeting *all* of my financial obligations" is a much more powerful message to your subconscious.

Your dream includes how you want to feel, what you are able to do, where you want to live, what your days look like, with whom you are spending them, and why this is all so important to you. You may have to look deep inside to identify your dream. If you've always wanted to go to India, but you have been telling yourself for years that it is too expensive, you will need to blow the dust off that dream in order to let it come true. When you turn your attention to how you want things to be, your focus, your energy, and your emotions work synergistically. The universe is now more apt to rearrange itself to help you get your prize. Let go and grab hold … all in one gesture. If you figure out what you really want and you help people get what *they* want, you will get back more than you bargained for. This will be among the best deals of your entire life. In network marketing you will meet people who are living the life of their dreams. *Why not you?*

Chapter Nine

◟

Focus and Discipline

"Success is focusing the full power of all you are on what you have a burning desire to achieve." ~Wilifred Peterson

My father taught me that a business is like a wheelbarrow. In order to keep it moving forward, you have to keep pushing it. The old quip about being an entrepreneur is that the good news is you don't have a boss. The bad news is that you don't have a boss. If things are going to happen, the buck starts and stops with you.

The first time I heard the following quote was from Jerry Clark. "Simple disciplines repeated over time produce massive results." It remains among those little ditties I have remembered countless times over the years. The success of your business will be as much a result of the small things you do on a regular basis, as any of the monumental projects you take on.

EXAMPLES OF SIMPLE DISCIPLINES

What are the steps that lead up to customers buying your products and associates joining your organization? What are some of those simple things that, when practiced steadily, produce massive results?

- Making one more return call before you leave your office for the day.
- Following up with a prospective customer or associate.
- Updating your dream board or vision statement to remind you what you are working for.
- Asking for a referral.
- Refreshing the items in your prospecting tool bag.
- Starting one more conversation with a prospect.
- Delivering that sample to a prospective customer when you said you would.
- Adding a message about your business or product to your e-mail signature.
- Updating your Web site with fresh content.
- Arranging for a promotional or educational event with your business associates.
- Setting up a blog to promulgate your message about products and services.
- Choosing a training call over watching TV.
- Creating "power hours" on a daily basis to focus on your business with no distractions.
- Making every segment of time count, from large ones like an entire day to a single minute.

It is so easy to avoid doing a task to advance your business because the consequence is not immediate. So what if you watch TV instead of reviewing a training CD? There is no immediate downside. What happens if you read *People* magazine instead of learning about the products you market? In the short term, nothing happens. Unfortunately, in the long term, likewise *nothing happens.*

The converse of Clark's message is equally significant: A simple lack of discipline repeated over time produces massive consequences. Not once, but repeatedly. Think about it. Make sure that you get both sides of this maxim. Put this into action to bring more profit, results, and satisfaction to you, the business owner. Value your efforts, knowing they count. This is especially important to remember when you see no immediate result.

It is important for you to get clear on what you want the results of your efforts to be. As a business owner, you determine the growth and direction of your enterprise. When your success in business is attached to personal benefits that *you insist on having in your life*, the consequences of your decisions are more apparent. You ascribe to "pay now, play later" versus "play now, pay later." The direct result is the quality of your life.

Most of what you will learn as an entrepreneur will be the result of simple disciplines. A year of doing extra little things can produce massive results. The math of this is simple. Let's say every day you choose to make one more follow-up call. You know when the time is right for this because you are about to pack up. This is the point when you flex your muscles of determination and pick up the phone or compose and send an e-mail.

This habit could result in more than two hundred and fifty additional follow-ups per year, allowing for vacations and days off. The fortune is in the follow-up. If nothing more changed in your business other than your doubling or tripling your efforts to follow up consistently, the results would be staggering. You would be destined to be counted among the high achievers. Your success can be fast and furious or gradual and steady, but your actions ensure that you are getting there.

Let's compare your success as a business owner to creating a healthy body. One day of no exercise will have no impact on you. You can easily justify taking a day off. But taking a month or a year off will have enormous consequences. One day at the gym or taking a long walk may not extend your life expectancy or improve your health. But getting a good workout several times per week over an extended period of time will alter the course and length of your life. Similarly, eating one piece of cake may have no impact on your body. But one piece every day for a week or every other day for a year will have a significant impact, and not a favorable one. Just as healthy people ask, "What body do I want to create?" successful network marketers ask "What lifestyle do I want to create?"

Successful entrepreneurs, like people who take excellent care of themselves with regard to their health, nutrition, and exercise, tell the truth about their focus, discipline, and determination. Whether it is a commitment to a healthy bank account or a healthy body, being honest will help ensure better results. It is too easy to talk the talk. In fact, those serious about getting results realize that paying lip service to succeeding in business or improving their health gets them nowhere. Talking about results without the concomitant action to produce them is simply a fabrication. Make your life about converting what you have declared as your intentions into reality. This is where the true value of your life emerges. Being in business for yourself provides the opportunity to experience that glorious satisfaction that comes with doing this over and over. Can you imagine how much power you generate by choosing results-oriented disciplines over time?

Can you imagine how much power you generate by choosing results-oriented disciplines over time?

When I was growing up, I was criticized for being so driven. As a result, I held back because I felt judged. On my fiftieth birthday I re-evaluated all aspects of my life; I questioned the notion that being driven was a flaw. The flaw was in the notion, not in being driven, I realized. Suddenly I saw clearly how blessed I was to be so determined, focused, and energetic in my pursuit of personal and professional development and financial freedom. All those years that shadowy presence had the effect of tamping down my enormous creative reserves. Uncovering that fact enabled me to finally break through. Understanding this was a defining moment for me in my ability to succeed in various aspects of my life. Might you have similar scripts that effectively deter your success? What lies between you and arriving at your next achievement level? What do you tell yourself about your capabilities? If you have any negative self-talk, might it be false?

Brian Tracy promotes being hard-working when it comes to running your own business. He says that those who succeed as business owners go to work earlier than everyone else and are still working when everyone has gone home. As a hard-working person, you are the one who gets it done. You learn to work more effectively and efficiently than others who are less determined than you are. You develop leadership qualities, you set better boundaries with others in order to get your work done, you continue to be more and more resourceful, and you relish the good feelings that come with being focused and disciplined. You appreciate the clarity of your mind and your ability to complete the most important tasks. You are a master at time management, and you get twice the amount done that most people get done in half the time. You are respected for your accountability, integrity, and professionalism. People admire you for your unwavering determination. You are at the helm of your ship knowing that this ensures that you stay on course. Drifting aimlessly is something you would never tolerate. You discover and embrace your inner drive that gives you energy and adds excitement to your life every day. You are among the happiest people you know. You have a very high attractor factor, and people are drawn to you. You inspire and influence others. *You make more money, you have clients and customers who buy more of your products and services, and you are a role model for others.*

Think of a high achiever who absolutely loves her work. Such a rock star helps raise the bar for all of us. She gives high achievement/high performance/hard work a very good name. Being a hard worker is a virtue. And except for those who inherit their wealth, it is also a necessity to produce complete freedom.

Whether you are brand new or you want to reenergize your already existing business, let yourself create little successes. Signing-up one customer would be an example. The energy you experience will help you get into higher gear, thus enabling you to create progressively bigger successes. If you will take those small but significant steps every day, you will gradually find yourself aligned with your purpose. You know what you want and what you deserve. When people see where you are going, some will want to go with you. If you take enough steps—even baby ones—if you don't stop, you will eventually arrive at your destination. One partner in my organization recently achieved a new leadership level within our company's pay structure. That accomplishment has done more for her in terms of her commitment and determination than anything else she has achieved.

If you take enough steps— even baby ones— if you don't stop, you will eventually arrive at your destination.

That little bit of extra effort on a daily and weekly basis can become the momentum for taking your enterprise and your results from good to great. Growth is vital. Granted, for those at the elite levels there may come a time when all of the lifestyle and financial goals have been met. But even among some of these super-high-achieving giants there is passion burning in the belly because of their love of the game. Those completely committed to the outcome are naturally inclined to do whatever is necessary, consistently, over time.

We frequently talk about working smarter instead of harder. In order to get to the place where you really are working smarter—which will be evidenced by your having more to show for less effort—along the way you will have to work differently from when you were compensated with wages. Until it all kicks in, staying focused might be quite challenging, and the amount of effort required may seem daunting. Using systems;

becoming more focused; attending to the most important tasks; and putting in the days, weeks, months, and sometimes years will ensure that you get what you came here for: a life of freedom. You must understand that what you are creating for you and your family *does* require a lot of work. This is natural because you are producing results that are potentially greater than anything you have ever done. Focus and discipline are their own reward and will pay you indefinitely.

Chapter Ten

~

Prosperity Consciousness

"There is a time to let things happen and a time to make things happen."
~ Hugh Prather

Are you clearly on a journey to become more prosperous? Are you moving smoothly toward your goals? Does it feel arduous to you at times? Dealing with your thoughts and beliefs might feel like wrestling an alligator. Many of the patterns in your thought process are firmly established, especially your beliefs. Could these beliefs make it harder for money and optimal health to find their way to you? One of the keys to your success will be your willingness to address these issues. You can only allow as much wealth into your life as you are prepared to accept. If you find yourself thinking negative, limiting thoughts, you have your work cut out for you. As you begin to enjoy thoughts and sensations that support your creating a life of abundance, you are well on your way.

The culture of network marketing encourages personal development in this arena because we believe that you deserve to be prosperous. For many individuals, this requires an inner shift in order to actually live a life of financial freedom. Most people were not trained to believe that there is an abundance of money and that it can flow endlessly. Since creating and sharing wealth is the heartbeat of this industry, a business model that is designed to give you a continual flow of cash also gives you the chance to examine your relationship with money.

FINANCES AND YOUR OPERATING SYSTEM

I met Maria on a flight from Salt Lake City to San Francisco. By the time we landed, I learned that Maria is wealthy by most standards. She owns her home free and clear. Her family is blessed with substantial resources. She has an excellent track record of creating a solid, six-figure income. Maria is smart, resourceful, and industrious. However, she was singing the blues about having insufficient funds. Her daughter was heading off to college, and Maria reacted with worrisome thoughts about not having enough money. In her own words, she was freaking out. The amount of money she had did not change, but her thinking process was derailed along with her perception. It was as if Maria had suddenly lost everything she owned since she was now focused on *not* having money.

This would be like sitting next to a magnificent garden with a wall between you and the beautiful plants and flowers. You can insist that there is no garden because you cannot see it. That does not mean that the lovely landscape does not exist, but it is "true" to you nevertheless. The wall in this case was Maria's imagination and what she was telling herself about her assets. Even though the garden (her resources) was separated from her experience only by the imaginary wall she had built, she still insisted that it was not there.

In her groundbreaking book *The Soul of Money*, Lynn Twist challenges the reader to examine his belief systems around money. The grand wake-up call in this book is to discover that what most people deem as insufficiency is erroneous. If people in third-world countries can experience wealth with one miniscule fraction of the material comforts that we experience every day, does that not put things in perspective? This shift in perception is the cornerstone to Twist's message. *Waking up to a fresh viewpoint about how plentiful the universe is can be the start of your journey that allows for even more.*

Learning to be able to see this garden every day, when that wall disappears once and for all, will be a function of your releasing your resistance to the inevitability of abundance. Abundance was always there, you will discover. Pay attention to what you focus on. Is it the wall or what is on the other side? Hopefully, as you gain awareness you can become sensitive to what awaits you on the other side, where the gorgeous landscape lies. The landscape represents wealth and prosperity, which you deserve. Any thoughts or beliefs to the contrary are lies that you have learned to tell yourself.

Money will go where it is most welcome and appreciated, like a guest in your home. The clarity of your invitation and the degree to which you are receptive will determine the amount of wealth you permit in your life. This is why I associate relaxation with abundance: pushing money away requires mental, physical, and psychological effort. Accepting wealth implies surrendering. It may appear that there is a lot of work that goes into creating abundance and affluence. But when it kicks in, you find that it is not only about hard work; it is also about allowing, relaxing, and receiving.

> Money will go where it is most welcome and appreciated, like a guest in your home.

You will become and remain wealthy to the degree that you align yourself with being a person of affluence. A classic example is someone who wins the lottery and loses the enormous fortune almost as fast as she won it. This is typically what happens when the recipient has not adjusted to this new level of wealth. There are various stages to permit wealth to enter *and remain* in your life.

- Get clear on *what* you want.
- Know *why* you want it.
- Know *how* this wealth will enable you to contribute in order to make the world a better place.

- Know beyond a shadow of a doubt that you deserve to be wealthy.

Network marketing will encourage you if you are seeking a way to manifest and enjoy wealth and the freedom that comes along with it. Spending time with a group of prosperous people will inspire you. The most successful and wealthy people in network marketing are the ones who have the biggest desire to help you achieve the same. In no other industry are the leaders more determined to teach you how to become rich.

It is life-changing to learn exactly how and where you want to spend your money. Then, when you have it, you can spend it with more joy because you have identified what is valuable to you. Let's say one of your most ardent desires is to leave a financial legacy for your children. *When you begin to invest in what you have deemed the most important way to spend your money, you can begin to feel good about doing so.* You are aligned with this aspect of spending your assets. Those good feelings support your having more.

THE MAGIC OF RESOURCEFULNESS

When your mind is relaxed, you may discover that you are more creative. This is why meditation is recommended as a way to help you get clear mentally in order to become more productive. Ideas can flow to you like a river when you are in a positive and open frame of mind. You can begin to listen in on your own creativity. When the background in your mind is quiet, you can sense and respond to these ideas. I know when I am in good shape mentally because I have exciting ideas for my business that flow copiously. Not all ideas pan out, but many of them do.

Lynn Twist recommends that we switch our frame of reference from focusing on our problems to identifying available resources. In so doing, what was always available in terms of prosperity, people, and power grows for the attention we place on it. Those who are the most resourceful will prosper and inspire others as well. One of my primary roles as a team leader is to continually learn how we as individuals and as an organization can create profitable businesses. Being resourceful is like having a full tank. I am responsible for my own growth and ongoing education in order to stay a step ahead of those whom I have the privilege of training.

It is important to monitor yourself when you become anxious or fearful. It is not a crime to be mentally stressed, but it does limit our connection with our own resourcefulness. I observe how fear and anxiety limit me specifically because of how the flow of great ideas is impeded. When we are resourceful, on the other hand, we are connected to our source, which represents an unlimited supply of everything we need.

> It is not a crime to be mentally stressed, but it does limit your connection with your own resourcefulness.

GIVERS GAIN

Abundance should and does include contributing to others. I have never had as much money in my life as when I started to give it away on a regular basis. Originally, I was taught that if I gave it away, there would not be enough left over. That is a startling example of a belief system that does not serve my desire for affluence. Lynn Twist encourages her readers to be so grateful for what we have as a *starting* point. She says, "What you appreciate—appreciates." If you claim that you want to live abundantly, but you find yourself focusing on your insufficiency, you have created a barrier between you and the money you desire.

Some self-proclaimed spiritual people live life on the edge of bankruptcy. It is one thing to live an abstemious life as a monk in a cave; renouncing worldly possessions may be virtuous, but it is not the path of most entrepreneurs. There is nothing spiritual about being limited financially. If you desire to live abundantly, yet you do not experience true wealth in your life, your spiritual work is not complete. It would be like having gone to the school of personal development and missing the entire semester that teaches you how to live a prosperous life. Some people find money "unspiritual." Nothing could be further from the truth. Some of your greatest accomplishments on your road to becoming a more fulfilled person will be supported by an increase of financial resources. Education, travel, and contributing to your family, a charity, or the environment—things that make your life more fulfilling—require money.

Perhaps you are drawn to network marketing because of your commitment to complete your work around health and finances. Do you know that there is a garden? Do you want to allow that wall to come down and disappear from the face of your world once and for always? Release any strain that causes a disconnection between your desire and your reality. Identify and challenge any erroneous beliefs of insufficiency. How do you recognize them? You will feel smaller and tenser when you perceive not having enough. Beliefs like this make your world seem less significant and possibilities limited. The converse, prosperity consciousness, entails excitement and joy. There are endless possibilities from this vantage point. You are more creative, more energetic, and more optimistic when you are connected to your positive beliefs about prosperity.

If you feel that an old guard is defending your beliefs about lack and limitation, turn to a new guard that reminds you continuously of the abundance in this universe and how grateful you are to receive, give back, and allow more. For example, if you look at your commission check from your network marketing business, can you see it for not only what it is, *but what it is becoming*? If you look at your check and feel bad because it is not big enough, you are pinching yourself off from a greater flow. Examine all of those reactions. Allow the physical reality around you to respond favorably and take notice. An attitude of gratitude is a gift you give to yourself.

In network marketing you can spend time with people who will be thrilled to learn about your dreams and your goals. They will demonstrate for you how to think differently about time, money, giving back, and freedom. Imagine a community of people who encourage each other and encourage you. You can follow and model these people as you attract others who will choose you as *their* leader. In so doing, you have a benchmark for some of the most significant work you will ever do in this lifetime. Wake up and smell the abundance. It is intoxicating, and it is okay to want more.

Chapter Eleven

✧

It Pays to Be Healthy

"The winners in life treat their body as if it were a magnificent spacecraft that gives them the finest transportation and endurance for their lives."
~ Denis Waitley

According to Paul Zane Pilzer, leading economist, author, and expert on trends driven by baby boomers, the wellness revolution is "the next trillion dollar industry." More than eighty million people born between 1946 and 1964 invest precious time, energy, and resources to look and feel younger. The science of anti-aging has come into its own with advances in medicine and complementary products, services, and techniques designed and formulated to prevent disease and to promote longevity and prolonged youthfulness. Now, more than at any time in history, health is everybody's business.

At the same time, we are witnessing an epidemic of degenerative diseases, many of which are environmental, lifestyle, and stress-induced. Annual deaths from these illnesses are in the millions. Certain ailments, such as cardiovascular disease, cancer, and diabetes are estimated to be up to 85 percent avoidable. Such authoritative institutions as the American Diabetes Association, the Harvard School of Public Health, and the Centers for Disease Control promote diet, exercise, and nutrition to help prevent one of the most epidemic culprits of all times: type II Diabetes. These sources suggest that with lifestyle changes, diabetes is up to 58 percent preventable.

We can add quality and years to our lives by paying attention to our bodies and taking care of ourselves. If your goal is to live a long and healthy life, you can follow the recommendations of such experts in the field of longevity as Dr. Deepak Chopra. In *Ageless Body, Timeless Mind*, Chopra discusses the benefits of maintaining a steady weight, remaining physically active, and eating in moderation. John Maxwell, an expert in leadership and a prolific author, worked himself into a life-threatening heart attack through stress and an unhealthy lifestyle. He now preaches that the smartest thing we can all do is to proactively maintain good health while we still have it. Maxwell believes that one of the causes of poor health is being over-worked, which itself is a stressor. From his own close call, he learned and now teaches that it is prudent to make our own health a priority early in life so as to avoid having to take our hard-earned assets to try to buy back our health once we have lost it. There is less emotional strain on your family when you take good care of yourself. It is cheaper, more convenient, easier, less of a hassle, and a lot more fun to remain healthy than it is to try to recover from being ill.

HEALTH, TIME, AND LONGEVITY

I chose a network marketing company that manufactures and distributes health-based products. However, the benefit of making our health a priority extends to other network marketers who focus on non-health-related products and services. Many people in network marketing are dedicated to personal growth and the development of leadership skills. If you are committed to self-improvement, by extension you would address goals, issues, and concerns around your health and your body. Being the best you can be and living a life that is about influencing others to improve *their* lives suggests that you find time to eat well, exercise regularly, and de-stress. It is more difficult to live a life of making a difference if your energy is chronically low, or if you hate the way you look and feel. It makes sense that you would make taking care of yourself a priority.

In our business, we preach the benefits of "work/life balance." This means that you have a favorable ratio of time for your business, time for your family, time for fun and recreation, and time to take care of yourself. Time is a "biggie" for many people. The belief that there is not enough time is insidious and will show up over and over during the day. Furthermore, it can take its toll on people who never get around to doing good things for their bodies. The perception that there is a shortage of time manifests for many individuals as they're putting caring for themselves at the bottom of the list. It never gets done.

Be careful what you affirm. Deepak Chopra has shown medical evidence that when we believe that there is not enough time we run the potential risk of having our lives be shortened. There are even disease-promoting biochemical processes in our bodies that speed up when we think we are going to run out of time. Be mindful of any thoughts and emotions on the topic of time, especially fearful ones. If you find yourself chanting during the day, "there is not enough time," you may be unwittingly creating undue stress and tension, which we all know is not good for you. There is actually a condition called "hurry sickness." It is the bane of people who are unable to manage their time and always fear that they are running out of it. The result is a release of stress-related hormones—which themselves are related to a host of lifestyle-induced diseases including hypertension and metabolic syndrome, a group of clinically measurable pre-diabetic indicators.

Learning to relax around how much time you have will give you more of it. For starters, without those stress-related hormones, you just might be healthier, which can translate to living a longer life. Your perception of sufficiency around time will alter your experience of it, thus creating a positive feedback loop. This is among many reasons why yoga is called the fountain of youth and why I continue to practice it and recommend it. Yoga promotes relaxation mentally and physically. By adjusting your perceptions and learning to relax, you can create "more than enough time" just as you created "not enough time." Your life may depend on your making this shift. The new chant gradually becomes "there is plenty of time." It will help you feel much better.

TAKE YOUR BODY WITH YOU

It takes energy and stamina to stay focused and productive. A fortified immune system is required to protect you during stressful times. The more well days you have and the fewer sick days you have, the more time you have to get the job done and enjoy the fruits of your labor. You want to be as healthy and energetic as possible.

It takes a lot of time and considerable mental and physical energy to manage being sick. Conversely, when you are feeling great, you are more apt to be productive and enthusiastic about life in general and your work in particular. Having radiant energy increases your attractor factor and will draw people to you. Some of the most important people you will ever meet and work with will find you because of your glowing good health.

I have told two little stories so many times that I have come to believe both of them.

- I am younger and healthier now than I was ten years ago.
- My health is so good that it will rub off on you.

Being healthy does not necessarily mean having a heart of a twenty-year-old. Nor does looking good require that you win a beauty pageant. And last, being fit doesn't mean you are going to place first in the Ironman competition. Putting these qualities in perspective can help you steer yourself to making choices that improve how you look and how you feel on a daily basis. The benefits will reward you now and for the rest of your life. Feeling better physically can catapult you into higher performance, higher earning, and being able to help more people.

If your goal is to build a thriving and profitable business, you will definitely want to maximize your energy to support you in achieving that.

You Are Who You Create

In all areas of health and wellness, focusing on the body you want to create can energize you more than any deprivation diet or New Year's resolution. When you are clear why you want to live—and when you have attached this purpose to the people you love and the lives you want to change—you are propelled forward. Asking yourself what you want to create holds more positive energy than telling yourself what you cannot eat or forcing yourself to do exercises that you hate. Stay positive. Have fun. Enjoy the creative process as you choose wellness every day.

> Asking yourself what you want to create holds more positive energy than telling yourself what you cannot eat, or forcing yourself to do exercises that you hate.

Here is an example of someone who got clear on the value to him and his family in choosing to be healthy. Mario is someone I met through my networking organization. His own father died in his fifties and never met his grandchildren, Mario's children. Wisely, Mario linked his own food and exercise choices with his most compelling reason to live a long life, which is to see his grandchildren grown. He lost the weight around his middle because he learned that central obesity was one of the strongest predictors of diabetes and cardiovascular disease. He began to exercise daily and adopted pro-health eating habits. He discovered the body that he wanted to create and attached a higher purpose to having it. For the first time, Mario did not have to deprive himself of foods that he knows are not good for him and that he used to eat guiltily. By getting in touch with the feelings and desires to enjoy his grandchildren throughout their lives, Mario's appetite for pro-health food kicked in naturally.

Mario said this was effortless compared to times in the past when he tried to lose weight while focusing on what he could not eat and feeling bad about himself and his body while attempting to make changes. He shifted his entire focus and enjoyed the creative process for the first time in his life. A surprising side benefit to Mario was that he got hooked on feeling relaxed and energetic in his body and wanted to perpetuate that experience.

If you wish to change your point of focus, a good starting point is your selection of meals and snacks and what you eat to sustain yourself. Think of this as the octane level of the fuel on which your body runs. Eating nutrition-dense food that is high in fiber, complex carbohydrates, and artery-friendly fats will improve your health. Dr. Ray Strand, MD, is a practicing physician, author, and expert in wellness and nutrition. According to Dr. Strand, avoiding processed foods, refined sugar, and saturated fat helps prevent a variety of illnesses, such as cancer, diabetes, and cardiovascular disease.

Adding quality supplements to your diet provides your body with extra protection to promote wellness and longevity. An immune system that operates optimally is one that receives the proper ratio and quantities of vitamins, minerals, and other micronutrients. A diet rich in antioxidants (through diet and supplementation) gives your cells what they need to function optimally. Since our cells are the smallest living building blocks in our bodies, they determine the way our bodies function on all levels.

When you have consumed whole foods and supplements that provide a broad spectrum of health-promoting nutrients, there is far less damage when you enjoy an occasional treat. When you are fortified you are not at risk, so you can afford to be imperfect. It is freeing to know you can enjoy little pleasures without compromising your overall wellness. We love dark chocolate in my family. When taken in moderation, and when we sustain ourselves on pro-health meals and snacks, we can easily tolerate a little sweet treat without undesirable consequences. So can you.

According to Dr. Strand, these are the benefits to you for the following:

Healthy Diet

- Weight loss
- Improved sensitivity to insulin
- Decreased risk of heart disease
- Decreased risk of most cancers
- Decreased risk of diabetes
- Decreased risk of Alzheimer's dementia
- Decreased risk of macular degeneration
- Decreased risk of degenerative arthritis
- Enhanced immune system

Exercise

- Weight loss
- Lower blood pressure
- Stronger bones
- Decreased risk of osteoporosis
- Improved insulin sensitivity
- Decreased risk of heart disease
- Decreased risk of diabetes
- Enhanced immune system
- Increased strength and coordination
- Overall increased sense of well-being

Nutritional Supplementation

- Optimized antioxidant defense system
- Optimized repair system
- Improved insulin sensitivity
- Strengthened body's natural defense systems
- Maximized protection for optimal health

FALLING IN LOVE WITH FOODS THAT ARE GOOD FOR YOU

There are countless reasons why people do not choose pro-health food. Do any of these look familiar to you?

- Not enough time
- Don't know how to prepare
- Can't buy stuff like that where you live
- Costs too much
- Your spouse and kids won't eat it if you feed it to them
- Does not taste good

When your intention to be well is high, whatever arguments you have made to defend your habits to eat unhealthy food begin to drop away. You have done many things in life that are far more difficult than adding fruits, vegetables, and whole grains to your meals and snacks. If you come back to "What do you want to create?" then your choices (and your body) change shape over time. Bring consciousness to what you put into your mouth. Pay attention to your emotions when you reach for food. Relax and breathe while you eat. It is important for you to be conscious of what you eat and how you feel when you are eating. Feeling centered, grounded, and relaxed around food will help you make choices that promote longevity, increased energy, and better health. Especially in our culture in which so many people are addicted to carbohydrates, the benefits to you of feeling calm and in control around food and eating are underrated. Your life is worth living fully. Making healthy choices is an extension of high self-esteem and your desire to be in control and to make a difference for others. Choose freedom over enslavement to unhealthy substances. Doing so actually promotes greater health because of the peace of mind this entails.

The most delicious food in the world is the food that is the best for you. For example, many brands of multi-grain pasta and bread are loaded with health-promoting nutrients. They have a heartier texture than those made with refined and processed flour that contain empty calories. Whole foods like these give you something to chew, and because they contain no processed sugar and flour they won't spike your blood sugar. This is called the low-glycemic approach to improved nutrition and better health. You may discover that foods like this provide immediate and lasting satisfaction. If you are more habituated to eating processed foods, I think you will be pleasantly surprised by the benefits to you of substituting nutritious foods for the ones you normally select. They naturally give you more sustained energy and help you feel better. As someone in network marketing, perhaps you have set big goals for your life and your business. Without the crash and burn effect and the tiredness caused by eating junk food and highly processed food, the foods I am recommending are better for supporting you in achieving your goals.

> Making healthy choices is an extension of high self-esteem and your desire to be in control and to make a difference for others.

Just as you do not have to become Mr. Universe to be in better shape, you do not need to overhaul your entire diet to improve your health. One of the biggest reasons why people do not make modifications in their diet is because they believe that it won't make a difference. This is erroneous thinking. You have to start somewhere. Focus on the incremental benefits as you allow for even greater ones. If you find one new pro-health substitute in your meal planning per month, at the end of one year you will have radically improved your diet. Something deceptively simple like switching from white to brown rice or corn tortillas to sprouted-grain tortillas helps.

What about those of you who are not currently engaged in a healthy diet and exercise program? There is hope for you as well. Let's say that Point A is where you are now. Point B is where you are headed if you continue on the same pathway.

Point A (poor diet, lack of exercise) ⟶ Point B (risk of chronic disease)

If Point B is not where you want to end up, you can make some modifications that are modest and achievable in their scope but potentially significant in their benefit. Let's say for dessert after dinner you replace ice cream with fruit. Add a thirty-minute walk a few times per week. If your body cannot handle thirty, start with ten and build up gradually. Let's throw in a daily regimen of high-quality supplements. You have now lowered your sugar intake, upped your consumption of fiber and antioxidants, gotten the glucose from your blood to your muscles (where it will be stored as energy rather than fat), and added a layer of protection to your cells—all with a modicum of behavior modification.

These simple disciplines repeated over time can produce dramatic results.

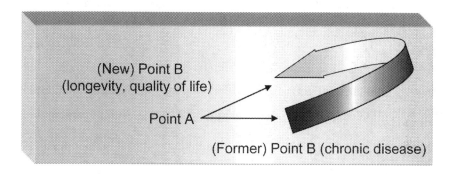

A few degrees in a different direction, *extended over time*, will draw you to a completely new destination. When it comes to your health, never underestimate the benefit of simple changes along the way. Every improvement you make counts.

MOVEMENT AND EXERCISE

Do you find time each day to live actively in your body, or do you find yourself making more excuses than you do exercise dates with yourself? Do any of these common justifications for not getting exercise look familiar to you?

- I don't have a buddy.
- I don't have the time.
- I don't belong to a gym.
- My body hurts.
- I look terrible, and I don't want people to see me.
- I don't have the right clothes.
- The weather is wrong.
- I don't like to sweat.
- I don't have the right equipment.

Like making better food and nutrition choices, finding a way to incorporate movement into your day will pay you dividends for a very long time. In my experience working with people who needed a boost over their resistance to exercise, once they get hooked on the good feelings that come with moving their bodies, it becomes more difficult not to go for that walk than it was to do it. People who get inspired by the joys of physical activity often grow to crave it. Whereas before they believed that there was no time, once a decision and a commitment are made, suddenly there is time every day to go for at least a twenty-minute walk. It is like throwing a switch. In fact, for those of us who enjoy the benefits of exercise and movement, we feel incomplete on a day that passes without it. Someone once asked me how I feel when I don't exercise. I said, "I don't know. I never wanted to find out."

Exercise is another component of living your best life. This entails moving, breathing, and getting your heart rate up. If you are like me and you have a lot of energy to burn, you may find that breaking a sweat will bring relief and will enhance the feel-good benefits of being active. If you suffer from low energy, you may discover that you actually acquire more energy once you start moving and breathing more deeply. This is why exercise is often recommended to help mitigate the symptoms of depression.

Being physically dynamic creates natural mood-elevating hormones and reduces stress. Because some of the hormones that are stress-related have potentially serious side effects, here you have a winning combination—exercise both improves your health and releases toxins caused by stress. The enjoyment factor and the health benefits can transform your day and brighten your outlook. A moving, stretching, breathing, and strengthening break will help you become more cheerful, more relaxed, and more optimistic. By creating a slower resting heart rate—which is the result of exercising and getting in better shape—you become calmer and more centered as you face challenges and take on bigger projects.

Make time to rest, recharge, and re-energize. You are worth it. You deserve to feel terrific. Once you get hooked on how you feel from something as simple as walking around the block a few times, you will discover that you look forward to moving your body and the relaxation that follows.

YOUR BODY AND UNFINISHED BUSINESS

Over lunch one day, a friend named Katy told me that her biggest fear is becoming like her mother, whose health was always poor. She, the mother, was dependent, needy, and a burden to her two daughters. Katy said that she wants nothing more than *not* to become like her mother. In a confidential manner, she told me how much sleep she loses worrying about her own health and fearing that she will die early. Katy is very overweight, which she knows puts her at risk for cardiovascular disease and diabetes, two conditions her mother has.

Katy is as an example of someone whose life is impacted by a misalignment with her body. She is accomplished professionally and holds a prominent position as a professor at a local university. Her work in education is recognized nationwide. By many standards, she is a high achiever. Amazingly, Katy has done all of this while simultaneously living in dread of her impending mortality and physical dependency. She is doing good work on the outside, but unfortunately feels miserable on the inside. In her own words, she is always stressed.

What is it about this highly accomplished individual that on one level is out in the world making a difference, and on another is terribly unhappy about her health and her body? Katy has done an impressive amount of work in her field, but she is sorely lacking from having done work on *herself*, particularly around her body. She is in her early fifties, suffers from osteoarthritis, recently had her hip replaced surgically, and in her own words, struggles every day. Although she is smart and educated, and although she knows the consequences of her choices, she refuses to make any changes that benefit her body or her health.

I have tremendous compassion for anyone who is out of sync with her health and her body. Many years ago, I myself was locked in a belief that supported my being ill. It looked from the outside that I was doing good work. But the struggle inside was very real and quite painful. Because I had not chosen to be well yet, years ago life was much more difficult for me than it is now. Because this was my experience, I recognize unfinished business in others. My life changed dramatically when I realized that being healthy was a choice.

My life changed dramatically when I realized that being healthy was a choice.

Is failing health inevitable, or might you challenge that belief for your own benefit? Imagine that your health can improve year by year. Be the best you can be in this body. As I did on my own journey, you will need to stare down any limiting beliefs you have about your health and your body as well as address certain changes you need to make. I do not mean to make this sound easy, because for me this was sustained personal work that took place over time. But it was among the most amazing and significant transformational experiences of my life.

Many of us have learned the value of creating strong and healthy bodies. We take our bodies with us on life's journey. When I remind myself what my purpose is—to improve the health of others, to create financial freedom, to leave a legacy for my children, and to help others achieve freedom—my choices are crystal clear. You too can put time and effort into your daily practice, through food choices, exercise, and supplementation. Once you discover the most compelling reason for you to do this, you may encounter less resistance and experience less of a struggle. This might be easier than you think.

Whether you are moving mountains or just climbing them, anything you can do to increase your vitality will support you throughout your day. If time management is the challenge, putting things on your calendar will increase the chance that you actually get to them. If you are super busy and work from a calendar or to-do list, schedule time for a walk or a yoga or dance class so you see it on your list. With practice, the thought that you are too busy to exercise is a cue to move, breathe, and work your muscles. After a great workout it can seem as if you bought yourself more time. You will come back to work refreshed and energized.

Getting hooked on feeling good is an excellent way to perpetuate new habits. Give yourself a gift and give yourself a break. Be well. The world will be a better place for you and those you love when you take good care of yourself.

Chapter Twelve

∽

You and Your Money

"Perhaps the most powerful single factor in your financial success is your beliefs about yourself and money." ~ Brian Tracy

During the recent global recession, perhaps you were one of those blessed individuals who found gold amidst the rubble. Over the course of history, incredible opportunities were the direct result of a downturn in the economy. Network marketing is such an opportunity.

As an entrepreneur, I feel that I have always been responsible for generating my income, during recessions as well as during booming economies. The conversation about building a network marketing business during a sideways economy may be different for two reasons:

- I get to help more people address their fears about work and finances.

And conversely,

- More people are open-minded to alternatives to traditional employment.

However, as a business owner, my own focus and determination are the same now as before this downturn in the economy. My friends who have gotten laid off are scrambling in ways I myself have never experienced. For entrepreneurs who are used to *causing* our income to perpetuate, we are used to navigating through unpredictable terrain.

Being a business owner in network marketing requires that you manage your money differently than people who work for someone else. Not only do you strive to maintain a steady stream of passive income, but you will be challenged and inspired by others to continually create abundance and prosperity in your life. Creating financial surplus—defined as having more than enough to do what you want to do when you want to do it—when you own your own business can be among the most satisfying experiences of your life. Oil tycoon J. Paul Getty said, "There is only one way to make a great deal of money, and that is in a business of your own." Disciplining yourself to work your business faithfully over time, in order to produce desired results and achieve your goals, will teach you to become stronger both within as well as outside of your business.

Voluntary frugality is a good money management skill. There is nothing wrong with tightening your belt. Even Suze Orman, the money guru, recommends that it is important to differentiate between wanting something and needing something, especially during a downturn in the economy. It is essential to have good spending habits in order to create wealth and manage your money well. The trick with frugality is to choose to live below your means while avoiding fear-based thoughts. Deciding not to buy something can be a mindful and deliberate act of preserving your assets. But pay attention to any thoughts of insufficiency, lack, or loss. One of the most important things I have ever learned was to say to myself, "I choose not to buy that now" instead of ever thinking or uttering the words, "I cannot afford that." Spending prudently does not preclude thinking prosperously. In fact, it may be a precursor.

> Understand the operating system that determines how you think and behave around money.

If each of our parents had a different set of beliefs (which mine did), then we are hybrids in our beliefs. No wonder so many people are confused. Insanity around money is potentially quite contagious. This is why it is so important to grow to understand the operating system that determines how you think and behave around money.

Spend time with people whose lifestyles and values you would like to emulate. Learning other ways that people think about money can have a positive effect on you. I was deeply influenced by people I met at seminars with Klemmer and Associates. The way they thought about and took action toward charitable contributions inspired me to take action in new ways. I found several charities to which I contribute regularly, and I feel grateful for having made those connections. Warren Buffett of Berkshire Hathaway says "It's better to hang out with people better than you. Pick out associates whose behavior is better than yours, and you'll drift in that direction." I would add that by extension, you will then attract people of a higher caliber who want to hang out with *you*.

A prospective associate named Marissa told me about her goals as a network marketing professional. Although she wants more money, prosperity is frowned upon in her church. In that community, people with money are judged as evil and selfish. Marissa and her husband are both hard-working professionals, but they are broke. No wonder. She will need to address her beliefs about money before she allows herself to succeed.

YOUR RELATIONSHIP WITH MONEY

Pay attention to your reactions to events that happen in your environment. During the recession that began in 2008, you had ample opportunity to find out what you are made of. In an environment in which many people are voicing their fears and concerns, your strengths and weaknesses will be more noticeable. If your beliefs in yourself are strong to the core, then you will always seek and find solutions and alternatives regardless of what is happening in the culture around you. I have never been more excited about my network marketing business than I am now. At a time when some individuals are practically scared to death about money, I get to work with people who are grabbing the golden ring and drawing themselves up to solid ground. The value of this business model has increased during the recession because for people who are looking for work, giving themselves work can be very powerful. Smart networkers are capitalizing on this trend, helping themselves and others at the same time. We see ourselves prospering now and indefinitely, regardless of what the economy is doing.

Some people will cling fiercely to old systems that have nearly deteriorated before their very eyes. It is difficult to say "job" and "security" in the same sentence with a straight face. Some very capable individuals will go out with their hat in their hand practically begging someone to give them a job. Because they are afraid to venture outside of their comfort zone, some people are unable to recognize the gift that a business like network marketing represents. On the other hand, when someone with whom we are speaking discovers the power and momentum possible through leveraged income and business ownership, we are excited to know that our message got through to him. We are discovering and creating an entire breed of new entrepreneurs who are willing to re-invent themselves in order to thrive. Paul Zane Pilzer, author and leading economist, actually calls this group "The New Millionaires."

In all times of history, there have been individuals who thrived, regardless of their external circumstances. Because of opportunities that had not been available before the Depression, some industrious and forward-thinking people emerged as millionaires during the worst downturn in our nation's economy. Owners of movie houses found themselves in the right place at the right time. They were able to make a lot of money while others felt desperate and hopeless. Wealth continues to be made; it is just distributed differently depending on the economic climate.

In present time, the Internet and social media have emerged as the self-appointed voice of the merits of network marketing during a recession. Those of us who have been working our businesses diligently over the years are thrilled by various credible news sources suggesting that there is a fresh new face of network marketing. This is third-party validation and not network marketing voting for itself. Steven Covey, business and leadership expert and author of *The Seven Habits of Highly Successful People*, said in an interview in *Network Marketing Magazine*, "I think network marketing has come of age. It's become undeniable that it's a viable way to entrepreneurship and independence for millions of people."

> We are thrilled by news sources suggesting that there is a fresh new face of network marketing.

By focusing on such positive messages, you can learn to control your emotions when fear and panic are promulgated by the masses. This is a good insurance policy for financial security. Even if your savings have temporarily dwindled in the stock market, knowing that these changes to your finances are simply happening, versus happening to you, will help you remain empowered. My business associates and I feel that our optimism and enthusiasm are as essential as our daily vitamins. One woman in my organization and her husband are out of work. Her determination to build wealth during this recession is inspiring. She is already saying that losing her job was a blessing in disguise. She is having more fun and is more optimistic as a business owner than she was in her previous corporate position, where she now realizes she was not in control of her economic future. Taking responsibility for her finances by giving herself work means no longer abdicating this responsibility or power to someone or something else.

People will rise up in any economy. The direct sales industry attracts some of the brightest and the most ambitious. People who are able to create financial freedom through a home-based business are in a position to lead and inspire others now more than at any other time. Robert Allen, the author of countless books on real estate and investing, is a staunch supporter of network marketing. He enthusiastically encourages his audiences to consider it as a workable path for dramatically improving their finances.

Allen says that there are two doors. One has security written, on it and the other has freedom written on it. For those who choose the security door, they will have neither freedom nor security. Those who choose freedom get both.

Trying to reach higher financial ground by depending on someone else to give you a job when that very job can be taken away by the person who gave it to you is, according to Allan, practically caveman thinking. There is nothing wrong with working for someone else. It is just imprudent to consider this a path toward financial freedom or financial security. Security is sacrificed when control is relinquished.

In his educational and inspiring book *The Flow of Time and Money,* Dr. Lloyd Watts explains how, in order to create true wealth and real freedom, we need to make our money work for us. In my networking organization we call this working for wealth, not wages. An understanding and application of the principles that govern how money and time are interwoven is the key to living a full and prosperous life. Watts' explanation of what happens when our money is put to work for us (rather than the other way around) is an inadvertent salute to network marketing. Watt's powerful message blends time and money into a single equation that must be understood by anyone wanting to live freely. The author provides an authoritative illustration—with words and diagrams—of what we are doing in this industry, which is why network marketers should read it. Watts says that many people have time *or* money; it is tricky to have both simultaneously. His illustrations and narrative support our premise in network marketing that you must create passive income in order to be free.

Make sure you know who is the slave, you or your money. Who or what works for whom? If you work for money, you cannot be free. You must continue to work if your system is set up to pay you once for your effort. For example, if you make a certain amount per hour, if you stop working, you stop getting paid. This is how I was compensated when I was Rolfing and teaching yoga, and also why I was so determined to make a change.

If your money works for you, you can command the flow by your deliberate efforts to increase it. In his infinite wisdom, Brian Tracy says, "You are not wealthy just because you earn a lot of money. You are only wealthy when your money works for you. To become wealthy, your main job is to acquire money and then put it to work making more money for you."

How to Get Paid in Network Marketing

In network marketing, a good compensation plan should address a distributor's financial goals with a systematic, calculable method for achieving them. For example, in my company's plan, a business center is a virtual store that represents an asset that is worth fifty-two thousand dollars of annual passive income when fully maximized (not including bonuses). Let's say your goal was to have approximately one hundred thousand dollars in permanent passive income. That would be two of those stores working at full capacity, paying you night and day with no break to your income. When you decide that you are going to work for wealth instead of wages, you can chart your course to complete financial independence. For the truly ambitious, making a half million dollars per year or more becomes a possibility because the math and the system are mapped out. Depending on the size of your dream and how determined you are, you can work toward maximizing as many business centers as you are capable of building. Your results will be a function of your vision, determination, and effort. It will also depend on how willing you are to learn the skills necessary to achieve whatever milestone you desire.

It is possible to create financial independence in network marketing during good times and bad times. The state of the economy has relatively little to do with this fact, something that can be said for few professional sectors. For practically 100 percent of the population, a "paltry" fifty-two thousand dollars of continual cash flow per year would be life changing. This represents even more significance in a downturn economy than when the economy is robust. Talking about freedom when many people are desperate to find work makes those of us who have chosen this path feel blessed. For anyone motivated and willing to lay the foundation, freedom becomes a distinct possibility. Whom do you know whose life would not be forever altered with an additional thousand dollars per week? Given the potential earnings of capitalizing on multiple business centers, this goal becomes comparatively mild.

The best way to make adjustments in the way that you think about money is through education and awareness. The entire series by Dr. Thomas Stanley is among the most illuminating I have ever read. *The Millionaire Mind* provides an insider's view of how millionaires relate to money. The millionaires who were interviewed said that it is important for anyone who wants to be in control of his finances to do two things: create leverage and gain control of his taxes. You can do both of these through network marketing. This message is the basis for another classic on the subject, *The Richest Man in Babylon* by George S. Clason, originally written in 1955. The message in the book points to the agelessness of the principles of acquiring wealth and becoming free.

EXERCISES FOR CREATING WEALTH

Beliefs about money affect decisions we make every day. Have you ever stopped to realize how many times during the day you evaluate things through the lens of what is affordable, what is the cheapest way to do something, how much something costs, whether something is worth the price, and so on? Consider the following exercises to learn more about how you relate to money, as well as what some of your beliefs and attitudes signify.

- Take out a twenty-dollar bill. Let it talk to you. What does your money say to you? "Don't spend me"? "There is plenty of me to go around"? "This is running out"? "I work for you"? "There is always more where this came from"? "If you spend me, you will be broke"? Let the face on the bill tell you some of your beliefs about money.

- Notice your thoughts when you take money out of your wallet to spend. Do you release it freely, telling yourself that more than that will replace it? What goes on inside your head?

- Notice your emotions when you take money out of your wallet to spend. Guilt? Pleasure? Altruism? Fear? Happiness? Faith? Notice if you feel tense or relaxed when you spend money.

- Notice how many times during the day you attach the *cost* of doing something with the mere *thought* of doing something. (This is a good exercise for people who say that money does not matter to them.)

- Notice during the day if you say no to doing or having something, *automatically* thinking "too much money" or "too expensive" or "can't afford."

- Notice your thoughts and emotions when you learn that someone has something that you would like to have or is able to do something that you would love to do. (If you appreciate that person for having or doing that thing, you are closer to being able to have or do things like that yourself. If you resent that person, you may be unwittingly negating *your* ability to do and have things like that. Allowing yourself to be inspired by another person's achievements helps move you to being able to achieve those things for yourself.)

- Pay attention to your thoughts about the future. When you visualize in advance short-term and long-term periods in your life, are you anticipating optimistically? Do you have any "default" expectations that preclude abundance and prosperity? What *are* your expectations? Are your thoughts and images about the future in line with your desires? (One prospective network marketing associate kept saying that she really wanted to start her business. When asked when that would be, she voiced her belief that not only was she broke now, but that she expected not to have any money in the future. I challenged her on this belief and worked with her to adjust it.)

- Can you train yourself to notice evidence of prosperity *on purpose?* Can you find proof of abundance and affluence on a daily basis? (Go to an upscale restaurant, ballet, or concert and notice the crowds of people enjoying themselves and the seats that are all sold out. Notice beauty and luxury around you and relax into the expectation of abundance in your own life.)

- Pay attention to what you say about yourself and your money. Are you programming yourself to create wealth? What comes out of your mouth as you speak about your finances and lifestyle?

- Do you hold back when you discover something you really want to do or have, or do you find yourself creatively planning for ways to achieve it? Can you open your mind to new possibilities? Can you see yourself attracting opportunities in order to be able to do and have the things you desire?

- When you spend, invest, or donate money, do you see it coming back to you in greater abundance? Can you release your money knowing that there will be ample returned to you?
- Can you create a running list and find one hundred things you would do with a surplus of money? By opening your mind to these endless possibilities, you will be more inclined to implement strategies for achieving them.

One story to illustrate the above is of a man in network marketing whose name is Robert. He said that because his second daughter was going to college he now had to tighten the belt and spend less. I pointed out that perhaps *in addition* he might want to open the faucet to let in more financial resources. Both positions stem from what he tells himself. Robert was holding on to what he has because he perceived that now there was going to be less of it. He *says* he wants financial freedom but is unwittingly pinching himself off from it by focusing on the lack of money. Opening the faucet allows him to match and possibly exceed this new expense. Plus it helps Robert to attune himself to opportunities he might otherwise not notice.

FINANCIAL FREEDOM: FACT OR FICTION?

Because our expenses tend to expand as our earnings do, for many people, making more money means having more stuff and maybe even more fun, but possibly no more freedom. Even if what comes with more money is altruistic, such as higher education, once this new level is reached, it must be maintained. Watts calls these "triggered expenses." Once they get accustomed to having more stuff and more fun, people are often just as tethered to the job in which more income is available than they were to the previous job. Sometimes this entails dependency on even two jobs. This is the dark side of linear increases in income.

If you are tantalized by the idea of becoming financially free through network marketing, you need to start off by making a few dollars. For example, if you have little or no savings and you live paycheck to paycheck, you will need to do a tremendous amount of inner and outer work to become financially independent. This can and does happen, and the result is that you will think and behave very differently. Achieving progressive goals is best. What start off as small, incremental commission checks will continue to grow as long as you continue to grow yourself. Your outer game is a reflection of what is going on inside of you.

> If you are tantalized to become financially free through network marketing, you need to start off by making a few dollars.

In order to become truly free and independent, you need the following:

- A supply of money that will finance your doing what you want, when you want, for as long as you want, without running out. Or …
- A system for generating income that, once established, automatically produces more money than what it costs you to live life exactly as you please, and does so consistently over time.

Bottom line: you don't have to work for money.

IN OR OUT OF THE BOX

Let's say that you lived where you wanted, drove the car you wanted, gave to the charities of your choice, supported your family the way you wanted, shopped where you wanted, traveled when and where you wanted … and all of that cost two hundred fifty thousand dollars per year.

Figuratively, let's say that ideal life can be contained in a box this size:

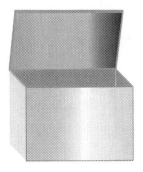

It should be noted that many people work very hard (often two jobs) with a *desire* for a life that needs a box the size of the one above, but make just enough to allow a life that is limited to this size:

This is when getting out of the box becomes a pressing reality for many hard-working individuals. The smaller the box relative to the size of the life you truly desire, the more you have to work. This is true even if you have a substantial income. If the two hundred fifty thousand dollars or more per year brings with it no time freedom, then you can be just as restricted as someone making a smaller salary. You might live in nicer surroundings and have nicer things, but the quality of your life is compromised if all you do is work.

Using the figure above, financial freedom would mean that an annual two hundred fifty thousand dollars of passive income comes to you automatically. The box created by the money that you earn is bigger than what is required for you to live as you desire. You now have more than enough. In a situation like this there is room in the box—which is your life—to express yourself, have fun, see the world, give to others, help your kids or your parents, relax, and enjoy living in any way you have deemed meaningful. Who wouldn't want a situation like that? These options are rarely if ever attached to traditional employment. You might not even believe that being free is within the realm of possibility if you worked all day and had little time or money at your disposal. I have a personal mission around this topic: When I meet someone who even mentions wanting to be free, I work very hard to help her understand how network marketing works. Why? Because for many people, the desire to be free can slip away as quickly as it appeared. If you had the fantasy to become financially free and no option presented itself, might you not give up on such a lofty desire? It takes effort to encourage someone to see that yes, her dream is attainable. I consider this to be one of my most important roles in building a profitable and stable organization.

Take Jacob, a personal trainer who believes he needs one hundred fifty thousand dollars per year to meet his financial obligations. He and his wife long to travel, in particular to Greece and South America, which is where their families originate. Jacob lives in San Francisco, where the cost of living is quite high. At fifty dollars an hour, which is Jacob's going rate, he would have to see sixty clients per week for fifty weeks out of the year to make that kind of money. And that is if he could even get that many clients. Even though Jacob loves his work, most likely he would get tired and perhaps burned out with a workload like that. However, with the income from a network marketing business, Jacob could have two streams of income: one from seeing his regular clients and one from residuals generated by his home-based business.

What does this mean to Jacob? He can build up his passive income in order to take back some of the time he used to devote to seeing his clients. Now he can travel with his wife without any loss to his revenue. Furthermore, he can work as a trainer for the love of it, on his own terms. Prior to enjoying his income from network marketing, Jacob had to work more than he wanted to or was able to. In the new situation, Jacob is able to release himself from the demands of his hourly work and set himself up to make money when he is not working. What a relief to him and his family. Also, passive revenue is like an insurance policy from any unexpected loss of Jacob's linear income.

Perhaps you are someone who absolutely adores your work. But even for the most passionate lot, maybe there are times when the income associated with your work either does not meet all of your expenses, or it requires too many hours, or it comes with too much pressure. This was my reality when I was Rolfing and teaching yoga. I loved it. But there were countless times over the years when I did it because I had to in order to make the money. I realized that if some of the money I needed came in residually, I could work on my own terms and be more selective about my clients, my hours, and my vacations. This is why I chose network marketing, to free me to do (or not do) this work when I wanted. With my network marketing business up and running, I now have reduced my practice to one Rolfing client, a marvelous woman whom I adore and see weekly when we are both in town. After more than thirty years, this is how much I want to do that work, and I am completely happy.

How about people who love what they do, but whose work simply does not support their ideal lifestyle? There are many people who love their jobs, but the money that can be made in their field is practically capped. For example, if a schoolteacher wants to make one hundred fifty thousand dollars per year, he will have to take a second job. Unfortunately, this usually creates more imbalances between time and money. With a network marketing income, once it is firmly established, the teacher can now do the work he loves while relaxing and enjoying the lifestyle he desires.

GETTING PAID OVER AND OVER

If you market an excellent product that is consumable, you will find loyal product users and distributors. Many of them will continue to use the products month after month, year after year. (I still have customers in my organization who began when I did in 1999.) What happens over time is that your base income becomes more solid. Let's say after a few years of part-time, focused effort your company puts sixty thousand dollars in your bank account automatically during a twelve-month period. Suppose that over the course of the next year, you actually make one hundred thousand dollars in income, which means you are working for 40 percent of your income while 60 percent of your income is automatic. Maybe a year after that, you are still working part-time, but your base (what comes in automatically) is now eighty-five thousand dollars, but your actual earnings will have increased to one hundred fifty thousand dollars. Being able to work to increase your base is one of the great benefits of network marketing. Each year, your efforts go into increasing your base earnings, which will potentially continue to reward you indefinitely as they grow exponentially.

The fact that this base is built with the help of a team makes it even more powerful. Even as your customers and associates come and go (and they will), your base increases with the new customers and associates enrolled by you and your fellow distributors. Some will become loyal product consumers forever, and some will continue to build their organizations with customers and new distributors. Congratulations. You are now leveraged.

In her insightful book *The Women's Millionaire Club*, Maureen G. Mulvaney created what she calls "The Secret Recipe for Success":

- Know what you want.
- Believe you can have it.
- Take action.
- Give thanks.

This formula can and should be applied by anyone who wants the financial and lifestyle benefits that were obtained by the women who are featured in Mulvaney's book.

Nathan is a man in my organization who is a rising star with our company. He left a lucrative job as an investment advisor for a large local bank in order to build his network marketing business. Nathan says he feels more in control of his finances now because he is able to work deliberately not only to replace but actually surpass his previous salary.

Before, Nathan had a lot of money, but he had no life other than working. Now he knows that he will never be fired, downsized, or passed over for someone younger or cheaper to do his job. Nathan's network marketing business partners encourage him to take time off and to stay healthy and relaxed, something that was completely foreign to him in his corporate job. According to Nathan, he has not made all the money he is going to make yet, but he is getting there. That's what we do. We take ourselves forward, one step at a time, in order to create the amount of money we need and want. We live in the realm of exciting possibilities on a daily basis.

Chapter Thirteen

◡◠◡

Leadership and Influence

"Do you realize how much your income and the quality of your relationships depends on your ability to persuade? Persuasion is the reason products are sold, businesses prosper, and relationships flourish."
~ Kurt Mortensen

A book on network marketing is not complete without a discussion about your ability to impact another's life. The word "leader" is used frequently to describe a network marketing distributor. It is important for you to understand the meaning of this word in this context and also how it is overused. Just enrolling another individual does not make you an automatic leader. Your ability to succeed in this industry is determined to a great extent by your embracing the authentic meaning of being a leader plus acquiring the skills to become one. You must have a strong desire to favorably impact someone else's life in order to build a sustaining, stable, and profitable organization. To that end, you must be willing to do the work that helps you get from where you are to becoming a person of influence.

Although it appears that some people are born with natural leadership tendencies, it is also a learned skill. One reason why some do not make it in this industry is an unwillingness to acquire those skills in order to become the person who leads others to change their lives. Conversely, the higher the degree to which a new associate takes this role on in earnest, the more success she will have in building her team of associates and customers. I address this topic with every prospective associate with whom I speak. I brief the newcomer on what we do and how she is expected to contribute to the team. We discuss openly what it will take for her to learn to spread a message of improved health and improved finances. Each member of this organization understands that in order for us to help her achieve her goals, she must be willing to assist us in touching others' lives as well. It is a chain reaction of people favorably altering the direction another person's life is taking. That is the force of leadership and the glue that holds a team together.

BECOMING A LEADER

To get better results in your business, you will need to invest time and effort in acquiring leadership skills. You may have to kick some stumbling blocks out of the way, which usually entail your beliefs about yourself and your attitudes on this subject. You may find yourself challenged and excited at the chance to flex your leadership muscles. It becomes easier and more natural as you practice your ability to influence others for their benefit. In leading others, your desire to produce positive change must be stronger than your concern about what people might think of you or even your fear of failing.

Each member of this organization understands that in order for us to help her achieve her goals, she must be willing to assist us in touching others' lives as well.

The ultimate benchmark is the caliber of people you attract and your ability to help them produce measurable results in *their* businesses and in *their* lives. It is exciting to lead people who are powerful in their own right. Influencing people with influence is thrilling because these people will connect with more influencers. By proxy, people of influence can lift an entire organization.

Simon joined the organization recently. He is a minister at a local chapel and has a full practice counseling couples and families. Because Simon has his own circle of influence, he has been remarkably successful at enrolling customers and new associates. Simon is a joy to work with. His natural desire to persuade people to take action for their own benefit has inspired others on the team. His new enrollees are eager to become more active because they are following a man whom they already know, respect, and admire. Simon said that it took him years to become the person to whom others turn for guidance. His willingness to capitalize on his hard-earned reputation *for the benefit of others* is what makes him such an asset to this organization.

Some individuals confuse personality types with the ability to lead. I know a few gentle souls who have wrestled with this issue in order to emerge as strong leaders. One woman named Pam discovered that her quiet nature did not preclude her ability to become a person of influence. She discovered an inner strength and an enormous desire to help other people. This might be a pivotal point for you if you are attracted to the benefits of this business model and the rewards that come from the personal work required for success. In my experience, the people who have grown and profited the most understand that their work is about helping others. In her gem of a book *Getting Out of Your Own Way*, Lynn Allen-Johnson states clearly that the path of leadership and the path of personal development intertwine.

"It's easy to make a buck. It's a lot harder to make a difference." Tom Brokaw

Network marketers often talk about getting out of our comfort zones. We realize that some of the best things in life are just beyond our reach and that we have to stretch to achieve them. We love this feeling. If you have not worked in an environment in which people all around you support you to be the best you can be, this might be difficult to imagine. We move forward by raising others up. We learn to hold others and ourselves accountable. The day you care more about making a difference in someone's life than you do about whether or not that person likes you is the day you have taken a step forward as a person of influence. I tell my fellow associates all the time: *My goal is to help you succeed. If you are pleased along the way, that is a bonus. But helping you get results is my number one objective.* Tom Brokaw said, "It's easy to make a buck. It's a lot harder to make a difference." How much value do you place on being able to help someone improve her life? The answer is commensurate with how much effort and commitment you will bring to the process of becoming a leader and succeeding in this type of business.

ELEVATE, DO NOT REDUCE

The chance to be an effective leader begins immediately during the prospecting process, when an associate is looking for customers and other associates. Let's say Bill wants to talk about his network marketing business with his co-worker Dave. If Bill makes the mistake of turning all of his conversations with Dave into an attempt to convince Dave to join his team, Bill has failed to honor Dave. He has put the relationship at risk by reducing Dave to a prospect and neglecting to attend to other aspects of their connection. These behaviors do not give network marketing a good name and do not support Bill in becoming an authentic leader. This is one reason why people are afraid that if they get involved, they will ruin their relationships with friends and family members. This is a legitimate concern if proper leadership skills are not taught to a new associate.

There is a more effective way for Bill to approach this so that he honors his relationship with Dave. When Bill talks to Dave about the possibility of working together, what Bill needs to convey is his willingness to *elevate* his relationship with Dave. To take what they have—namely a co-working relationship—and add to that the possibility of working and playing together on another field. Since this field happens to be exciting, dynamic, and professional, Bill's invitation to Dave should give Dave the feeling that Bill is genuinely interested in sharing this privilege with Dave. Since this field might be bigger than the field represented by their current job (which is often the case when you go from traditional employment to being your own boss), the tone of this discussion is much more exciting than when Bill was trying to convince Dave. Bill has invited Dave to be part of one of the most rewarding and meaningful parts of his life. Dave now feels honored, which will favorably impact his receptivity to Bill's invitation. Bill's behavior is much more fitting of a leader. Leaders inspire; they do not coerce.

Leaders inspire; they do not coerce.

WRESTLING WITH JUDGMENTS

As you become a leader, you will find yourself learning from someone whom you may never have considered as a person who had something to teach you. One of the biggest mistakes I made early on was to let my judgments prevent me from receiving valuable lessons from some people whom I deemed unworthy to be my teachers. I was wrong. Eventually I found myself gratefully sitting at the feet of people who did not have as much education as I have or who did not conjugate their verbs as well as I do but who had much to teach me. In many aspects of network marketing, they had far more experience and wisdom than I did. I am urging you to avoid making the same mistake of allowing your judgments to cloud your ability to be trained. Why should we expect that a leader be perfect? We will not be perfect even as we develop our leadership abilities. This is not about becoming perfect; it is about becoming influential.

At her company's convention, a networker named Ethel saw someone on stage who did something that she did not like. As a result, for two years Ethel sat sanctimoniously with her negative opinions about this one person and used those judgments as a justification for not approaching people to build out her network. It is a fatal mistake for you, as it was for Ethel, to let your opinions of others prevent you from learning from them. Surrender your ego by being willing to be trained by people who may not fit your picture of a leader or teacher, but who have much to offer you. The person who benefits the most from this surrendering is you.

Yesterday I spoke with a chiropractor who has worked his way to a high rank in his network marketing company's leadership program. On the phone I found him to be abrasive and aggressive. He interrupted me before I could finish a single sentence. I made a mental note to avoid speaking to people the way he spoke to me. It occurred to me afterward that perhaps others will experience him as energetic and enthusiastic. The point is, on the path to leadership you may discover that what used to bother you in people now becomes more of a non-issue. Your experience of someone does not define that person. Nor does someone's experience of you define you. This is incredibly freeing. Drama and judgment drop away when you can have your experience of someone and *move forward*. Doing just the opposite, namely focusing on her judgments, was precisely what caused Ethel to discount her company for two years. This behavior prevented her from succeeding. She had a story about the imperfections of her company's president, but she had no results to show in her business.

Business Not as Usual

If your experience comes from a work environment in which competition and backstabbing are the order of the day, you may find yourself somewhat disoriented in a leadership-based culture. An associate named Arlene said that in her former high-tech company, she felt that she put her heart into her work and it was given back to her as hamburger. With her network marketing company, she now experiences love and encouragement in a way that was completely unfamiliar to her. She came to the business initially with a determination to fight her way to the top and resisted all of the training to become a more effective leader. This was all she knew from corporate America. She finally burned out because that behavior is not tolerated in this business. She was encouraged to genuinely focus on helping others. Fortunately this very capable woman allowed herself to recalibrate to a new way of working cooperatively on a team and went on to be quite successful. Instead of edging people out, she now strives to move others forward.

Successful network marketers set very clear boundaries regarding with whom they can and cannot work. The mark of a good leader is that he will be too busy, literally, to overly focus on others when they are petty, whining, or more focused on excuses rather than results. As strong as is his desire to assist people in being able to have more, do more, and be more, his commitment is just as strong not to make his life about the negativity and complaining of people who refuse to budge. Among the most life-changing lessons I have learned is to distance myself from people like that. In the early days, I made the mistake of lowering myself in a vain attempt to help people fixated on grievances, complaints, and victimhood. I felt then as if I were stepping in quagmires. My life—and my business—changed dramatically as I learned to refuse to play a game that was smaller than the one I wanted my life to be about.

Focus on the strongest leaders in your organization. Leadership entails moving as many people forward and up as possible. In addition, being an effective leader necessitates releasing individuals who appear to be determined to bring themselves and others down. It serves no one—neither the team leader, the team, nor the individual—for an associate to make her life about getting someone to take action, move

> Leadership entails moving as many people forward and up as possible.

forward, think positively, and have a clear vision, when that person has no interest in any of those.

This business is 100 percent about people. Relationships evolve into friendships, or vice versa, and then develop into partnerships. The goal is leadership. Sometimes the friendship comes earlier in the sequence, but the objective is the same. It is your ability to convey not only the business but also the vision of network marketing that will enable you to find other leaders for your organization. In *The Twenty One Irrefutable Laws of Leadership*, John Maxwell states: "When people respect someone as a person, they admire her. When they respect her as a friend, they love her. When they respect her as a leader, they follow her." How will you know when you are a leader? Others are following you, and you are able to make a difference in their lives.

LEADERSHIP: A TWO-WAY STREET

The most successful people in an organization are more interested in doing exceptional work with measurable results than in merely looking good. These people will bring forward everything they have in order to succeed and grow. They are a joy to be around. I have joked often that the people on my team who have been the biggest contributors have attached siphon hoses to my body and have extracted every ounce of leadership juice they needed in order to succeed. I did the same with my upline leader and mentor. People who are determined to succeed demand excellence from their leader, which in turn encourages more growth and competence on the part of that leader.

Network marketing is an environment in which people expect the best from each other. When my mentor forgets to return a call, I call her again. I take responsibility. Gone are the days when I (wrongly) complained that she was not a good leader. What an error in judgment that was. I ask new team members to meet me halfway in communicating via e-mail and phone meetings. I ask them to take responsibility for their businesses from the start. Although I cannot guarantee that I will not make mistakes along the way, I have their best interest at heart, and my recommendations come from what I believe will best serve them based on my experience and their goals.

On occasion, leaders are known to take grief from others in their organizations. I have witnessed people who work the hardest for others be mercilessly sabotaged by those they were trying to help. In talking with friends from other lines of work (teachers, corporate employees, therapists, engineers, nurses, doctors), it is clear that network marketing is not unique in finding an occasional bad apple. What is unique is that we all work for ourselves; the rules are not enforced by a boss. It is in this culture—people working *with* each other rather than *for* someone else—that we find a self-governing approach to business. We set boundaries. We do not put up with people who are not team players. We focus on people who want to succeed individually and collectively. Leaders facilitate growth and development for others. In his must-read book for anyone in network marketing, Tom Barrett in *Dare to Dream, Work to Win* describes a capable network marketing leader as being like a head waiter, the one who works the hardest to ensure that everyone in his group succeeds.

The smartest associates build stable, profitable, and sizable organizations, modeling for their team members along the way how they can do the same. Mentoring and modeling work better than managing. If someone is unresponsive or disinterested, the leader must move on to work with those who are genuine in their ambitions and commitments. Hilton Johnson, MLM coach, said it perfectly: "You generate more business by focusing most of your time and energy on the strong and independent people in your group instead of the weak and needy."

Mentoring and modeling work better than managing.

REINFORCING THE CHAIN

Each new associate learns from the beginning that she is responsible for the development of her own organization. In a solid team, the support is incredible. A new associate discovers quickly how much help is being offered and how smart she is to accept it gratefully.

When an experienced and competent associate extends a hand, the newer associate should accept that gift without hesitation. This means several things.

- The new associate becomes part of the team by accepting this treasure of mentoring. It is so essential to the nature of this business that to disregard this piece is like breaking the chain. Teach your new associate that she will be led by others who are more competent and more experienced than she. It is in the interaction between seasoned associate and newer associate that the bond is formed that hopefully becomes a lasting and mutually profitable business partnership.

- By connecting with the experienced associate who offers to help and guide, the newer associate participates in the culture that will eventually be passed down to her team. How can she know how to pass the baton if she doesn't accept it from those who have come before her?

- Each associate follows the leader until she is leading the followers. This is the tradition of network marketing. This is what is often called "duplication."

Here is an example of leadership in motion. Suppose a seasoned distributor named Brenda has successfully brought many competent members to her organization. If Brenda is willing to make presentations for her team, she can contribute by helping those in her

> The leader is responsible for modeling and teaching the most essential skills. The associate is responsible for studying and practicing them.

organization to enroll new members. Anyone who witnesses this will model this behavior to the extent that he is willing to acquire the skills necessary to step into this role himself. If he is not determined, he will position himself as a follower, which will limit the degree to which he can build his team through his own efforts. If he is determined, nothing will stop him from duplicating the skill of actively enrolling others on his own. This dynamic is ongoing in a network organization. The leader is responsible for modeling and teaching the most essential skills. The associate is responsible for studying and practicing them.

Lead by example. Effective leaders are willing to be observed by others. The spotlight on leaders explains why people are inspired by their action. For those of us who like the accountability aspect of having a leadership role, this visibility is a litmus test of our integrity. It is a standard to live up to and a way to create the highest measure for ourselves and our organizations. The more you lead, the more eyes are on you.

Become the associate you want to attract to your organization. Do not expect anything from your team that you would not be willing to do yourself. Ask yourself every day if your actions, if duplicated throughout your organization, would produce results and profit for others whom you are leading. It is incumbent upon the enrolling sponsor to set the stage so that leadership attitudes and practices are understood by and attainable to the new associate.

You Can't Please All the People

In 1985 I had the honor of delivering the keynote presentation to the California Massage Therapy Association. Attendees filled out anonymous feedback forms that were then sent to the presenters. When I read the forms, I experienced a defining moment that has impacted my ability and willingness to be visible as a leader and influencer for all these years. The responses from those who attended my lecture and completed the forms ranged from "Her skirt was too short, I couldn't hear a word she said" to "I would follow her anywhere and take any course she ever offered." I took the feedback seriously. I also realized that all I could do and the only thing I had power over was to bring forward my best effort and my best work. The rest was not in my hands.

The way people experience you is to a large extent out of your control. Even if you do your absolute best job and your intentions are pure, some will appreciate what you do and some will think harshly of you. If you are a leader of integrity and dedication, some will want to model your behavior for the inspiration you provide, and others will want to find any excuse to cut you down. In network marketing, coming to terms with this is liberating and can launch you to a higher level. This is one of the core functions of leadership.

Leaders understand that someone who experiences a world of lack and insufficiency can feel threatened by someone else's success. It's as if there was a limited amount of success so that if one person has it there is less for someone else. It is critical for a leader to remain detached from those projections and to remain centered and effective in helping the associate to understand his erroneous and limiting beliefs and attitudes. This is when the leader's inner strength comes into play. She cannot help someone who is caught in his scarcity mentality if she, the leader, allows herself to be reduced in this interaction. This is a time when the leader has an opportunity to facilitate significant change and development on behalf of her associates.

A good leader continues to push the edges of her comfort zone many times. She speaks from her own experience when she tells someone in her organization that the comfort zone is overrated. She knows, also from experience, that doing things that are frightening—such as speaking in front of a group—does not destroy her. In fact, branching out from behaviors that were familiar but perhaps limiting—such as dreading to pick up the phone to follow up with a prospect—becomes easier as she gets braver. As a leader, she encourages people to put one foot in front of the other, thus empowering others to follow in her footsteps.

Competent leaders ask of their associates the same tough-love questions that they pose to themselves. Good leaders have a knack of creating dialogue that helps people get in touch with their own greatness. A skilled influencer knows *not* to say, "So, why can't you do this?" but rather, "What strengths will you need to muster in order to accomplish this?" Instead of "Why has it taken you so long to sponsor a new distributor?" she would say something uplifting, such as, "What are you doing every day to find your next distributor?" Such questions may take countless forms. The leader will bring the associate to higher ground through persistent and positive reinforcement.

Leaders know how to steer someone away from things like self-pity, insecurities, and self-doubt. A leader understands that someone's performance to a large extent is influenced by what the person thinks about his own abilities. To that extent, a competent leader can help the associate focus on that which will support his achieving his dreams and goals. A successful leader in network marketing who has helped others succeed must be willing to challenge a story that another person is telling of his own inadequacy. "Are you able to see yourself on the other side of that limiting belief?" "Can we work together in order for you to kick that stumbling block out of the way?" "Are you open to reconsidering that way of thinking?"

> A successful leader in network marketing who has helped others succeed must be willing to challenge a story that another person is telling of his own inadequacy.

As Brian Klemmer says, "A positive leader interferes in other people's lives and causes them to do what they otherwise would not do toward what is important to them." This often entails helping people change the way that they think.

In network marketing the one who influences the most number of people to reach for a better life is the one who succeeds. There is no shortage of winners in this game because each gives birth to other winners. It is contagious and exciting, and sometimes it requires nerves of steel to stay in the game. A top earner in this industry calls this "living your very best life." Such a path of self-discovery leads to personal and financial freedom. The stakes are high, the rewards are astonishing, and for many of us, it is a life-changing endeavor.

Chapter Fourteen

∽

Now That You Know

"Your imagination is your preview of life's coming attractions."
~ Albert Einstein

The most recent person who joined my network marketing organization is someone who told me when we met that in his previous career he had never worked so hard in his life and made so little money. His name is Frank, and he is in the slipcover business. As a thirty-plus-year veteran of the furniture and decorating industry, Frank has observed that the opportunities to do the work that he has done for a long time appear to have dried up. This used to be a profitable business for Frank. With recent changes to the economy, there is very little demand for what he does.

When I met Frank, he was feeling overwhelmed, disheartened, and unsure what to do. With two sons in college, and only his dwindling slipcover business revenue to pay for their tuitions, Frank felt that he had a real problem on his hands. He asked me about my network marketing business because he had always been intrigued about this industry.

It took some concerted energy and effort on my part to help Frank understand how a network marketing business might be a solution to his problem. As we got to know one another and spoke openly about his goals, Frank's outlook became brighter. He became hopeful that there was a way out of his dilemma. I mentioned to him that one of the bonds that strengthen those of us committed to our network marketing businesses is working with others who want and need answers to challenging financial predicaments. The formula reflects one of the most famous quotes made by the great Zig Ziglar: "You can get anything you want as long as you help enough people get what they want."

Once Frank was able to put his challenges in the context of a reason to help other people, he decided to become a member of the organization that I continue to build to this day. The chance to help himself by helping others lifted Frank—and his spirits—to higher ground.

There is an industry word that we call our "why." It is another way of naming our motivation. Those with the biggest "why" often build the most thriving organizations. There is a quirky aspect of network marketing; when our "why" gets bigger, we congratulate one another because we recognize this as a greater reason to get better at helping other people get what *they* want. Frank has what I love to call a big, fat, juicy "why." What Frank finally realized is that just as he was able to help people in his slipcover business, he now has an entirely new breed of prospective clients. As the number of people who want their furniture recovered has dwindled, the opposite can be said of people who need and want relief from the financial pickle in which they find themselves. There are so many people just like Frank, it is staggering to consider. Frank now has a new business and a renewed faith in his ability to bring his family to greater financial stability.

THE BIG TAKE-AWAY

I offer this story as an earnest attempt to do for you what I was able to do for Frank. I would like to support you as best I can to weigh the pros and cons of whether network marketing is the right step for you. Since no one has a crystal ball, the future is unknown. However, when you weigh the upside potential with the downside risk, you might draw the same conclusion as many people around the world have done who understand this fundamental truth about the work we networkers do. There is so much to gain, and so little to lose. Whether you decide that this is for you or not, at the very least, I hope you see that the risk-reward ratio is potentially quite favorable. That is among the most unique benefits of a business like this. Since you do not have to spend a lot of money, and since most of your financial outlay goes to products that you have identified as being high quality, right there you have minimized your exposure and risk. As I write this, some friends of mine are courageously and heroically building a business in the home construction industry in the Pacific Northwest. To start their business, they borrowed *ten million* dollars. My hat is off to them for their commitment, courage, strength, and vision. But when I compare that to a business with a start-up cost that is somewhere between the price of a nice dinner out and a laptop computer, I am reminded of and grateful for the relief this business has provided for me and my family for over ten years. If you will stay the course and acquire the skills, I suggest that through network marketing you are not at risk, especially relative to other career and business choices you could be making.

What about the upside? What about the chance to make friends and find strengths you did not know you have? How would you like to be supported by other people with whom you share a vision? If the work you are doing currently does not contain the potential of changing lives, let me tell you how exciting it is when I go to work on my business every day. If the work you are doing does not enable you to vacation without losing your income, again let me encourage you to experience this for yourself. There is an old saying that money does not make us happy. Some have replied, with wry humor, that they would prefer to experience this for themselves. The same can be said of freedom. Imagine that during an economic downturn someone is committed to helping you rise up financially and help others do the same. The secret is out. Now you know why network marketers may be an impassioned group. We are driven to help people understand what we do because we feel that we are put on earth to help those who need a boost.

There is a woman in my organization named Virginia. She is a financial planner by day and a network marketer by night. The group of professionals that she has assembled in building her organization is comprised of attorneys, realtors, and businesswomen who admitted that they needed help. Virginia has been able to communicate to these creative and resourceful individuals what they could accomplish by working together. This particular organization continues to grow because people are invited to participate in and also be inspired by a culture of helping others.

Don't get me wrong: this is not a business only for people who are in dire straits financially. On the contrary, in fact, some of the strongest members in my organization are affluent and already well established professionally. I was at the top of my previous career financially when I was first approached in 1999. Why, you might ask, do people like this get involved in network marketing? The answer is two-fold. First, success-oriented people can spot a viable business model that has the potential for producing considerable financial returns. They see it as a great investment to get their money working for them. And two, perhaps more importantly, it feels so darn good and it can be so much fun to work with people who are willing to reach for a brighter future that they do this for the personal reward it brings. And I will tell you a little secret: many of these people who are on solid ground financially do not have freedom. Thus, even *they* have much to gain.

Here is what you or anyone you know can gain from working in this industry:

- There is the possibility of something grand that could happen for you lifestyle-wise.
- You can acquire knowledge that could make a difference for you for the rest of your life. Sharing this information with

people whom you know and love could do the same for their lives. These are gifts that you can pay forward indefinitely.

- You could make friends with some of the most dynamic and inspiring people you will ever meet.
- You will be encouraged in ways that you may never have experienced before.
- You will be supported by people who want the absolute best for you and your loved ones.
- You could change your financial destiny.

I will ask you what I asked Frank right before he decided to become a network marketing business owner. Has anyone stepped forward offering you as much encouragement as I have? Most of you reading this are people whom I will never have the pleasure of meeting or working with. However, I know in my heart that lives will be changed because enough of you will see the possibilities and will take a leap of faith. In 1999 I simply started my business; I took the first step. Someone I knew and trusted said that this might be a great opportunity for me. And then I got lucky; I fell in love with this way of working. I stayed the course and allowed my life to be transformed. Will this happen for you? Neither you nor I have any idea. But what if you *do*, what if this *is* a chance of a lifetime? The only way to know is to take the first step. Now that you know, the choice is yours. The rest of your life awaits you as well, plus all of the possibilities that have been offered to you.

Part Two
Resources

Chapter Fifteen

Business Leaders on Network Marketing

The preeminent magazine that supports the industry of network marketing is *Networking Times*. Its publishers, Chris and Josephine Gross, are dear friends of this industry. They work tirelessly to keep the profession up to the highest standards. It is in part because of their generosity and ongoing vision that many of us feel as if we have found a career worthy of a lifetime of giving and changing lives.

You will be moved and inspired by the quotes below. It is a brilliant compilation of the thoughts of some of the most credible leaders on the American landscape of business, finance, coaching, and leadership.

This segment is a word-for-word replica of an article that appeared in *Networking Times* in May 2009. It is reproduced with permission from Gabriel Media Group, Inc. Full-color reprints of this article are available at *www.NetworkingTimes.com* and *www.NetworkMarketingIs.com*.

"Network Marketing Is …"
American Thought Leaders on the Network Marketing Profession

Last fall, as Wall Street blew up and the economy melted down, a number of large network marketing corporations posted some of the largest sales figures in their history. Even as millions of people saw their savings evaporate and stock portfolios disintegrate, network marketers worldwide were quietly taking stock of their businesses and asking, "Are we okay?"

In the main, the answer appears to be a cautious yes: network marketing historically has been to some extent countercyclical, faring relatively well at times when the economy at large does poorly. Still, to find adequate comparisons to the economic panic of today one has to look back to the 1930s—a time when network marketing had not yet been invented. So how are we doing?

For this issue, we assembled a panel of American thought leaders to give us their thoughts on the state of the profession. The consensus: our current economic woes may well bring about a historic upsurge in the popularity of the network marketing model.

—John David Mann, Consulting Editor to *Networking Times*

JOHN ASSARAF

Many people have the wrong idea of what network marketing is; the truth is that the business has evolved significantly in the last twenty years. There are those who will shy away from network marketing because of its past, and then there are those smart ones who will make their fortunes because they can forget the past and see the future.

In network marketing, the power of your connections and determination allows you to build a highly successful business without the traditional costs of going into business on your own. The products, systems and ability to generate a great income and lifestyle make a powerful combination for those who want their share of the American dream.

John Assaraf, co-author of the *New York Times* bestseller *The Answer*

Bob Burg

What I admire most about the noble profession of network marketing is that one succeeds only by helping others, by adding value to their lives—and for that matter, adding value to the lives of many. I also love the fact that anyone with a big enough desire to better their lot can succeed in the business if they are willing to work hard, and be consistent and persistent.

The network marketing model in conjunction with a high-quality product or service presents an unparalleled opportunity for people to thrive. In this economy? Perhaps *especially* in this economy.

Bob Burg, coauthor of the *Wall Street Journal* bestseller *The Go-Giver*

DC Cordova

Network marketing is the most innovative system for the twenty-first century of connectivity, networks and relationships. Obviously the marketplace is ready for it. Done correctly, it's a win-win for all concerned.

DC Cordova, CEO of Excellerated Business Schools

Stephen M. R. Covey

To me, the most interesting dimension of network marketing is the focus on building relationships of trust. All parties must be able to trust one another, or nothing moves forward. Accountability, transparency and other high-trust behaviors clearly flow out of your character and competence, which in turn help to improve, solidify and create better relationships. Those relationships are powerful fruits that enable you to enjoy greater collaboration, a better reputation and shared accomplishment.

When done well, network marketing is the speed of trust in action.

Stephen M. R. Covey, author of the *New York Times* bestseller *The Speed of Trust*

MICHAEL GERBER

Network marketing [provides a] purely democratic, highly entrepreneurial, deeply authentic and simple model for successful living. In network marketing, your success or your failure is completely up to you … [In network marketing,] you're not in the business of simply selling products or a business opportunity; you're in the transformation business.

Michael Gerber, author of the *New York Times* bestseller *The E-Myth*

SETH GODIN

Network marketing works when it's not about you. It works when it is about the customer. Not sort of about the customer as a way of helping you, not kinda about the customer when you imagine how they could act like you and become part of your downline. No, it works when it is generous and transparent and true.

If someone buys from you because they are a friend or because it's easier than avoiding you, that's not about the customer.

Here's my dream for you: find a product and a price and a story that people choose to seek out. Discover a niche that people would miss if it disappeared. Offer an experience that's about more than money, more than making a living and more than recruiting a new salesperson. When you bring joy, utility, and trust to people (at a fair price), they'll embrace you.

Seth Godin, author of the *New York Times* bestsellers *The Dip* and *Tribes*

SEN. ORRIN HATCH

During these difficult economic times, there is no doubt that the entrepreneurial spirit of network marketing companies and its sellers helps keep the American dream alive. It is this same spirit that will lift our country out of our current economic crisis. The hard work, tenacity and boundless energy of our country's direct sellers never cease to amaze me. We need you now more than ever.

Orrin Hatch , a six-term (and current) Republican Senator from Utah and former Chairman of the Senate Labor and Human Resources Committee

Ivan Misner

Though we cannot control the economy, we *can* control our response to the economy. Networking can keep your business alive and well during an economic downturn; you should never let a bad economy be your excuse for failure.

During the last recession, I watched thousands of businesspeople grow and prosper, because they made a conscious decision to refuse to participate in a recession. They succeeded by developing their networking skills and learning how to build their businesses through word of mouth—an important key to success and the most cost-effective form of advertising there is.

While others are looking at problems, those of us looking for opportunities will not only get through a bad economy but will prosper.

Ivan Misner, author of the *New York Times* bestseller *Truth or Delusion?* and founder of BNI

Nido Qubein

Network marketing rewards human potential, individual effort, collective support and positive action. It is a magnificent form of living free enterprise, of experiencing success and significance, and of enjoying the fruits of victory. It is also a way of growing as you prosper, a way of learning as you serve, and a way of sustaining recurring income as you live.

Nido Qubein, president of High Point University and chairman of the Great Harvest Bread Co.

CHRIS WIDENER

In today's economic uncertainty and turmoil, network marketing has become an even more viable option for those who want to be their own boss, earn a substantial full- or part-time income, and find more time freedom to pursue the things they really love in life. Now more than ever, you can take your future into your own hands by starting your own business and earning substantial profits rather than relying on traditional wages determined by someone else.

Chris Widener, author of the *New York Times* bestseller *The Angel Inside*

Views from Past Issues

The following are excerpts from interviews conducted over our past seven years of publication.

VIC CONANT

As good as the products are in network marketing, they are really secondary to the personal development. Go to any network marketing convention: what are they talking about? They talk about the freedom they're enjoying, the fabulous growth they're experiencing, how wonderful their relationships are, how much they're learning about life and about themselves.

It's not the supplement or the skin cream that did that. Sure, in many cases, you do have life-changing products. But what's really changed is their entire life. (Oct 02)

Vic Conant, president and CEO of Nightingale-Conant Corp.

PAUL ZANE PILZER

More than any other business, network marketing starts with the core: not with the product or the service, but with helping other people by teaching them how to succeed, regardless of their education or what business or field they've been in.

What's so exciting about network marketing is that you can offer this opportunity to anyone, and people can maximize the value of their life experiences instead of having those life experiences limit their opportunity. (Aug 03)

Paul Zane Pilzer, author of the *New York Times* bestseller *God Wants You to Be Rich*

SHARON WILSON

People who are attracted to network marketing tend to be more open; they're already "outside the box" thinkers, looking for a better way … a way that gives them a better sense of balance. This goes hand in hand with an inquiry into more spiritual values.

I think network marketing provides a fertile ground for spirituality. The concept of network marketing itself is all about creating an opportunity for collaboration, for win-wins, for everyone achieving their dreams. (Aug 03)

Sharon Wilson, founder of the Coaching from Spirit Foundation

DENIS WAITLEY, PhD

Network marketing is a tremendous way to cross boundaries and eliminate prejudice. This business offers an opportunity to transcend cultures, geography and even belief systems. It gives you the opportunity to deal with your global neighbors around the common idea of being more self-determined. It gives you the opportunity to eliminate or at least sidestep hierarchies—politics, ethnicity, culture, any barriers—and do business with one another, directly and globally. It doesn't really matter whether you speak the language or whether you eat differently or pray differently. (Jan 04)

Denis Waitley, author of the *New York Times* bestseller *Seeds of Greatness*

BRIAN BIRO

The beauty of network marketing is that if you are an effective coach, if you really do build people and help them break through their fears, it becomes a complete circle of success. You feel great, they're going to do better, that feeds your business and your income—and you're also providing a model for this person, who's now also going to become a coach.

You don't have to be the most articulate; you don't have to be the most educated; you don't have to be the greatest speaker. (Apr 04)

Brian Biro, author of *Beyond Success*

CAMERON JOHNSON

In the past few years, the model of affiliate marketing and click-through plans has helped legitimize the model of network marketing for a whole new generation. Network marketing is huge. Word of mouth is the best form of advertising. (Jul 04)

Cameron Johnson, author of the international bestseller *You Call the Shots*

DAVID BACH

The simplicity of network marketing is that you find something you deeply believe in, then use it yourself and tell other people about it.

I believe God put each one of us here to do something special. Most of us aren't doing whatever it is we were put here to do, because we're living paycheck to paycheck. Network marketing is a chance for you to make a little extra money, and with that, to buy your freedom. Do that, and you'll spend the rest of your life doing what you were put here to do. (Mar 05)

David Bach, author of six consecutive *New York Times* bestsellers, including *The Automatic Millionaire*

Robert Kiyosaki

Network marketing teaches basic, critical life skills. It teaches people how to overcome their fears, how to communicate, and how to handle rejection and maintain persistence. This kind of education is absolutely priceless.

Here's what I tell people: "Even if you don't like it, stay with it for five years and you'll be better equipped to survive in the real world of business. And you'll be a better person."

The people who are successful in network marketing have a spiritual cause. They genuinely want to help better others' lives. If you don't have that, if you just want a paycheck, then work for the post office! (Mar 05)

Robert Kiyosaki, author of the #1 *New York Times* bestseller *Rich Dad Poor Dad*

T. Harv Eker

The unusual and wonderful thing about network marketing is that everyone around you is working to help you grow, instead of trying to keep you down! In what other business do you have people making $50,000 and more a month—and they're willing to tell you exactly how they did it? (May 05)

T. Harv Eker. author of the #1 *New York Times* bestseller *Secrets of the Millionaire Mind*

Scott Allen

Network marketing has so obviously been such a successful business model, there's a good deal here that mainstream networkers can learn.

The top network marketers know that the three-foot rule is not what you do. If there is a three-foot rule, it's this: *Anybody within three feet of you is worth getting to know a little better.* (May 06)

Scott Allen, coauthor of *The Virtual Handshake* and is Entrepreneurs Guide for *About.com*

FRANK MAGUIRE

I believe America's economic future, the health of its commerce and service, is rooted in effective network marketing. People are sick and tired of the deprivation of human dignity they experience at the hands of so many of today's corporations, which in the past ten years have scooped up all the quid for the guys on top, leaving behind some very talented people without a future.

Network marketing is turning off the spotlight of working for a corporation, and turning on the floodlight of the greatness that we all have within us. I love what you're doing in network marketing, because you're creating an opportunity to affect the self-esteem of many, many people. You're giving people hope and providing a launching pad for them to discover their own greatness.

I think network marketing is potentially the greatest economic opportunity that has ever existed. (Sep 06)

Frank Maguire, a former senior executive of FedEx, KFC, ABC, and American Airlines

JIM TURNER

The significant thing that people often miss about network marketing is that it's in the vanguard of a major consumer movement, in which consumers and producers are merging and becoming the same thing.

In a way, multilevel marketing companies are the first generation of what Alvin Toffler calls *prosumers* [producer-consumers], because the marketing network is also the customer network. Every individual produces and consumes; it's like breathing – exhale, inhale. The more balanced you can be in production and consumption, the better your life is. And the more people who are balanced that way, the better the society is.

There are now some fifteen million people in network marketing [in the U.S.], and this is making a huge difference in the maturation of what it means to be a consumer, because you are by definition playing a more involved role in the production/consumption cycle.

If you made this the leading story of what multilevel marketers are doing, it would really help fuel the further growth of the community. And in doing so, you could easily become a significant part of the majority of households in America. (Nov 06)

Jim Turner, Esq., co-founder of Swankin & Turner and chairman of the board of Citizens for Health

BOB PROCTOR

The beautiful thing about network marketing is that it is the most moral form of compensation there is. And it follows the very best income-earning strategy: you're leveraging yourself and you're providing great service. You're waking people up. You're showing people how to spend their days doing what they love to do, while at the same time earning an excellent income.

Properly executed, network marketing gives people time and money freedom. It gives them liberty, which is their birthright. (Mar 07)

Bob Proctor, author of *You Were Born Rich*

BRAD SUGARS

The reason I think network marketing is the best business for so many people is that you don't have to learn *everything* about business to start. You don't have to learn production, shipping and so many other aspects of business. You've got to learn sales, marketing and team-building. If you can get those three things down, you'll be all right.

Your first year in network marketing is your apprenticeship. If you don't make any money in your first year, who cares? You've spent a year learning the trade. (Jul 07)

Brad Sugars, author of *Billionaire in Training*

BARBARA MARX HUBBARD

I like network marketing because, at least to some degree, it transcends the current competitive system. It's about *synergistic* leadership, that is, leadership that facilitates and empowers rather than dominates and controls.

I don't think we're going to have peace if we don't piece together the emergent potentials of our system. The pieces need to be networked—and that brings us back around to network marketing. I think it is prefiguring global intelligence. (May 08)

Barbara Marx Hubbard, author of *Conscious Evolution*

GREGG BRADEN

Every species in nature benefits from cooperation. When they behave cooperatively, they consistently produce more offspring, live longer and live more successfully. And [researchers have] found the same thing within indigenous human populations throughout the world: longevity and quality of life increases when they cooperate in the gathering and sharing of food, water and other resources.

The same principles apply in business: the more we can cooperate, the better we'll do. That's what network marketing is all about. (Jul 08)

Gregg Braden, author of the *New York Times* bestseller *The Isaiah Effect*

DR. LEONARD LASKOW

Network marketing is really about love. What makes network marketing more successful and in many ways more efficient than many other forms of marketing, is that it's based on one-to-one relationships.

Most successful network marketers sooner or later recognize the role of connectedness or relatedness—which is to say, love—in network marketing. The top people in networking are very much in touch with their hearts.

The heart's intelligence is the recognition of the oneness and the unity of all. If a business is going to be successful, it's ultimately going to have to come down to recognition of unity. (Nov 08)

Dr. Leonard Laskow, author of *Healing with Love*

Chapter Sixteen

~~

The Compensation Plan

Network marketing attracts people who want to be in charge of their lives. As associates we use the tools and resources to build a business in order to help us achieve our goals and desires. We employ leverage and work with a team of like-minded business partners. *Time and money become our allies.* This is significant in a world in which people are frequently deficient in one or both of these commodities. In network marketing, we work for financial independence, not wages, and we value our freedom to live life on our own terms.

It starts with the compensation plan. Plans vary from one company to another. People succeed working different plans within different companies; there is no one plan that you must follow. It is useful, however, to understand the pros and cons of your company's plan, since you will be using it to profit in your business. Plus, you will need to explain it to others. As an example, the following explanation is based on one such plan, the binary. This particular plan is based on the power of two, hence its name.

Within the plan I am using as an illustration, a new associate starts his business with a training kit that costs about thirty dollars. The details of this starter package will vary from company to company, but in general, this will get you a position in your sponsor's organization. Next, you select products for your personal consumption. This "inventory" is used to open your virtual store. You can choose items just for your own use, or, if you like, a broader range of products to share with your family, to give as gifts, or to use as samples for future customers. You and your sponsor will discuss the different options for your starter package. This is your initial cost, and it is a one-time investment.

Within about four weeks your own selection of products will be shipped to you from your company, and this will continue on a monthly basis. All associates in network marketing use or consume their company's products in order to qualify for commissions. This makes sense because being a product user yourself enables you to recommend them based on your own experience. In the binary plan, all of the products have a point value. Imagine every associate's products' points going into a giant kitty. It is from this kitty that commissions are drawn. In order to draw from the kitty in the form of revenue, each associate must contribute points to the collection of points along with the entire organization. Ideally, the amount of points each associate contributes is a tiny fraction compared with the amount of revenue he draws from the pot.

All of your ordering will be done online. Most associates just receive an automatic shipment that they can control or change any time they desire. Except for the basic monthly requirement, all other purchases count toward commissions. The more products purchased from your and your associates' virtual stores, the more commissions you will make.

What is the first thing that you would do if you had a store? Get customers, of course. In this binary plan example, your store looks like this: you, plus two customers:

When your customers buy from your store, you make money. Unlike a brick-and-mortar store, yours is an online store. You help your customers get the products from the same place you do, by ordering from the company's Web site or by phoning customer service. The parent company ships products directly to your customers' homes. Some associates choose to buy products and resell them for a profit. Others choose not to mark-up their products and prefer to help their customers "buy direct" from the company. As many other associates do, you may choose this option because there are several distinct advantages: You do not carry inventory. You do not handle money. You do not have to deliver products. There is no waiting period for your customer to get the products or for you to get paid. Your customers can get their products for the same low price as the one you pay, which is below wholesale. Many distributors are not necessarily interested in making a couple of extra dollars in reselling the products. When the products are more affordable to your customers, and they are loyal buyers, everybody wins. That means more quality products for your customers and more commissionable points for you. Think *volume*.

When your customers buy from your online store, all of their purchases are connected to your account and you get credit each time they make a purchase. Naturally, you may attract more than two customers. Let's say that you have six customers. Your business would look like this:

If you knew you were providing excellent products, do you think you could get six customers over a year or so? If you have chosen a well-run company, the skills required to do this successfully will be taught to you. One of the keys to remember here is that unlike a traditional retail store, in order to be profitable you will not need hoards of people coming into your store every day.

It will take some energy and effort, but with the help of your coach, surely you will be able to find a couple of people who are motivated entrepreneurs. These people will be come part of *your* marketing team. You will teach them to follow some simple steps, just like the ones you took: buy products (which they consume), help people become customers of their store, and along the way, find a few motivated people who want to join them and be part of *their* team.

Now your store has other stores connected to it. It looks something like this:

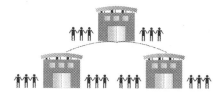

The exciting part of this is that *all of the customer purchases in the two new stores ring the cash register in your first store.* This godsend of an income model is perpetuated throughout your organization, as well as throughout the organization of everyone who has been enrolled on your team. Everyone's cash register rings when any customers shop in any of the stores throughout anyone's downstream organization. As organizations continue to grow exponentially (as associates enroll customers and other associates who in term do the same), the wealth potential of this model starts to kick in.

Now that your two new associates have each found six customers, your store now has twelve additional customers plus the merchandise purchased and consumed by the two new store owners. What did you do to have those twelve new customers be added to your total customer base? You showed the two new store owners how to relay information about the products to their customers and how to facilitate the transaction so that *their* customers (like your customers) acquire products directly from the parent company. Once you teach your new business partners how to relay information about the product, they can bring new customers to the network whether you are working or not. You are now leveraged, which is essential to getting time and money to work for you.

Let's go a few more layers down. You have your original store, which is now connected to a group of other stores. All of the business that happens in all of the other stores is funneled to your original store. Your organization might look something like this:

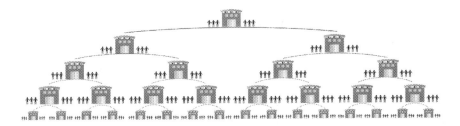

How does this build leverage and residual income?

- Your original store can be financed by an unlimited number of other stores that become part of your network.
- Once your organization is well established, your store can remain open and you can profit whether you are working, playing, traveling, or sleeping because of the activity in all of the other stores.
- Between you and the distributors on your team, the number of customers shopping in stores throughout your organization is potentially unlimited. In fact, the entire plan works beautifully when everyone in your group of store owners maintains about six or so customers. (This number can vary, and I am not suggesting that you stop at six customers. Six is used as an example. The company with which I work requires a *minimum* of five customers per distributorship.)
- You are entering the league of the wealthy: you are leveraged. *You are earning profits beyond your own expenditure of time, money, and energy.* When you are leveraged, you can produce

more with less effort than if you had to work for all of the money you wanted and needed to earn.

- If you are ambitious, you can have more than one store. In fact, you can have as many stores as you are willing to work toward. Let's say that one store, when operating at full capacity, is worth about sixty thousand dollars per year. Let's say, as an example, your ideal salary per year was two hundred thousand dollars. This is the income of between three and four stores operating at full capacity. From how many stores do you wish to be paid? The answer to this depends on how much you want to earn and how willing you are to develop the necessary skills to succeed. This is among the most attractive features of this plan. You are in charge, and you set your own salary based on your own effort. Want more money? Open another store!

- Your operating expenses remain relatively fixed even as your fleet of stores proliferates. You still eat your overhead. *When you put a new store in your network that you own, now the sales from your new store* also *ring the cash register of your first store.* Do you know how computers can talk to one another in a network? The same thing happens with all of your stores. They are connected.

- Network marketing attracts people who are self-starters. This keeps the energy of the group high. Working with professional people of integrity who are eager to help you succeed is often a refreshing change from working for someone else, or working for yourself without the support of a team.

- You can accomplish great things with part-time, focused effort. Since everybody is busy, by building a network of associates and customers, everybody is leveraged off the efforts of everyone else. For example, you might go to work for ten hours per week, but you'll have one hundred hours per week of productive time contributed by ten other like-minded associates in your organization, each working for ten hours that same week. When these busy people show other busy people how to get themselves leveraged, your organization continues to grow beyond your own efforts.

- You have created a legacy in which your efforts benefit your loved ones even when you pass. In some network marketing companies you can will your income to your children, spouse, or anyone you so desire.

Can you do it? It's up to you. The best way to determine your future is to create it. Does the system work? Absolutely, *if you implement it!* Are you looking for work? If so, you have come to the right place. Are you looking for a second stream of income? Through this plan you can keep your day job and work this as a part-time business. The person who will become your sponsor will help you see what you need to do in order to reach the goals you identify. Don't wait. The best time to plant a shade tree was twenty years ago. The next best time is now.

Chapter Seventeen

The Network Marketing Gene

This article appeared in *Networking Times Magazine*

Have you ever wondered if some people have the ability to succeed in network marketing programmed into their DNA, as if they were born to be good at this? While others seemed genetically challenged to make even some money, much less to reach the top of their company's pay plan. If there is a network marketing gene, does that suggest that perhaps there is a network marketing birth defect?

In my previous life I had a career that spanned three decades. At about the five-year mark I recall vividly thinking that I had really gotten the hang of my craft. Then, over the next twenty-five years, I continued to sharpen my saw. In my seventh year as a professional networker, the same is true: I no longer feel that I am prospecting, enrolling, and training in the dark. The experience of proficiency is not to be confused with knowing it all. It does mean, however, that the initial push up the learning curve has become less arduous. In both careers I performed very poorly in the beginning. I hold that experience of having moved from beginner to seasoned in another field as a template to guide me through the trials and tribulations of building and leading my networking organization.

The first career was a long and exciting one. I got so proficient at what I did one might think I was born to do it. But having inched my way to the top and having failed many times along the way, it is hard to say which was my greatest asset on my road to success: nature or nurture.

Most adults and many young people have mastered something in their lives. Parallels can be drawn from these different experiences, even in diverse fields. What are the common threads that appear in our various endeavors of going from novice to expert?

- Perseverance
- Acquiring new knowledge
- Learning from mistakes
- Motivation
- Having a goal, an objective, or some measurable outcome
- Capitalizing on our natural assets and overcoming our limitations.

THE SCIENCE OF SUCCESS

There is a science to getting really good at something and part of that is being bad at it at first. *In our business you don't have to be good to get started, but you have to get started to get good.* Everyone in our industry who has ever gotten really good at something can look back on the steps taken in another endeavor to go from being a beginner to becoming accomplished and apply that to their network marketing career.

Each new distributor comes to the team with strengths and challenges. Someone may be a whiz at the computer, personable and motivated, but who has unfinished business regarding her health which must be addressed on her way to success. How about someone who is smart, professional, has an enormous circle of influence, highly motivated, but who never acquired good listening skills along the way? These plusses and minuses come in an infinite assortment.

As leaders we must observe these assets and liabilities in order to guide our partners to achieving their goals. We teach our teams to fully utilize their natural, "genetic" abilities. And we work with the challenging areas so that they become growth opportunities and stepping stones. Just as everyone is challenged in different ways, the precise path to success is different for each individual.

Here is a little ditty that might get you through a tough day of collecting your yeses and nos. *It's not always easy, and it is always worth while.* When I thought I was going to perish from the effort of building a thriving organization, I leaned heavily on my previous experience of having woken up after five years in another gig really knowing what I was doing. I knew that feeling would come and I knew it was worth the time it took to get there. Are there experiences in your own past from which you can draw? Can you duplicate your own tried and true recipe of taking yourself through the paces of mastering a craft? Using those previous experiences as a compass, you might feel relief and confidence as you develop your new business skills.

THE OTHER DIMENSION

Through his seminars, Brian Klemmer of Klemmer and Associates (available at *www.klemmer.com*) teaches thousands of network marketers that there are two things that tend to run our behavior.

- Protecting our image
- Having to be right

In business building, these two tendencies are as insidious as an unpaired electron scavenging as a free radical. I learned this when listening to one of my partners describe a prospecting encounter in which she asked the standard question: *If time and finances were not limited, what would you do with your life?* When relating this story to me, the distributor obviously was a tad smug, knowing that she had asked the right question. After a little digging, it became apparent that there was no follow-up and no meaningful conversation with the person to whom she had asked this question. She succeeded in asking, but she neglected to understand the reply. This would be analogous to going to Barcelona, with the ability to ask perfectly in Spanish the whereabouts of the post office, but being clueless to decipher the response.

Our businesses will not be built on technique alone. Relationships are not built with prospective business partners solely as a result of saying the right thing. The metaphors for the quality of relationships we seek to create are often body based:

- Something you feel in your gut
- Heart to heart
- Belly to belly
- Eyeball to eyeball
- Getting under someone's skin
- A meeting of the minds

Once you say the right thing, the next step is to be present enough, with enough awareness, to make some real contact. Network marketing is not two dimensional. The third, critical dimension comes from your core. Helping people is not a throw-away term; we must walk our walk and close the gap between what we say and the real life results we achieve in touching other's lives. Is there a gene for success in network marketing? Yes, I think so. But it is not pre-ordained and it is not in short supply. We bestow it to ourselves. Natural talents plus sustained personal growth over time equals a shot at becoming one of those successful networkers who look like they were born to do this.

Chapter Eighteen

❧

Aligning Yourself with Success

Network Marketing Celebration Presentation
September 20, 2008
Santa Clara, California

We are what we think ...
All that we are,
arises with our thoughts.
With our thoughts
we make our world.

The Law of Attraction has been around for a long time. In fact, the proponents of it claim that it is ancient. It is a huge body of knowledge, made popular by the movie *The Secret* that was released in 2006. The quote above was made by the Buddha around 500 BC.

The law of attraction states that like attracts like. Successful people attract successful people. People with money attract money and people with money. Great opportunities find people who are open to receiving and recognizing them. One of the first things I learned when I got started in network marketing was to become the associate I wanted to attract. This was my first lesson in the law of attraction.

There are two components from the law of attraction that help us become better aligned with our success in building our businesses. These will be the focus of this talk.

The first segment is: The story you tell.

The second segment is: The thoughts you think.

Let's explore the first, the story you tell.

Have you ever found yourself beating the drum of what you do not want, only to discover that you get more of what you do not want? Do you hear yourself chanting over and over the problems in your business, with your downline, the lack of leadership, and the insufficiency of your commission checks? In this case, someone who continually tells the story of what she does not want is unwittingly attracting more of that to herself. Think of it as deepening the groove in a record.

Successful people chant songs of their successes. These are the songs all aspiring business owners can learn to sing. It is like repeating the words to a song over and over until they are etched in our consciousness and play like the default tune.

A long time ago I was part of a spiritual community. We chanted for hours a day. You probably know what a mantra is. The repetitions of this sound, or of these words, imbed the vibrations they contain deeper and deeper into our consciousness. This makes them more real. Imagine starting your day, faithfully chanting the familiar refrain about not having any good prospects. Wouldn't that make it harder to find and attract good prospects that day?

To align yourself with your success, tell the story as you want your life to be. There is an enormous array of data in your experience. What you focus on will have an impact on the reality that you create. Does it serve you to tell everyone about all of the distractions in your life? To beat the drum of not having enough time? To affirm that you don't have enough money? Do you think it might be hard for money to land on you if you keep saying that you don't have any? Can you see how money will be more attracted to you when you are grateful for all that you have, knowing that you allow even more? In the past, before I understood these principles, I used to whine to my friends about not having enough money. I had proof that there was not enough! I am grateful that those memories of the chronic dissatisfaction I experienced live snugly in the past, where they belong. When I learned how to focus on abundance, suddenly there was a lot more of it.

Like what happened to me, you can control how you feel and learn to feel much better by crafting a new story about the life you long to live. *Change your story, change your point of attraction, and let the universe rearrange itself.*

You are better aligned with your success when you focus on the evidence of having what you want. Bring your attention and your words to that story. There will always be distractions. But focus on a time when you experienced true abundance, even if it was just for a moment. There are always unexpected gifts. Tell the story of what a grateful recipient you are from an infinitely abundant universe. What you focus on becomes greater in your experience. As you focus on a different story, as you lean into the reality that you are in the process of creating, that reality is now attracted to you. This helps you find more joy and more ease in allowing your desires to become real.

No more demanding of the universe the life that you do not want by repeating the details of it incessantly. Get clear on what you *do* want. Gently demand of the universe to deliver that experience to you by aligning yourself through this new story that you are telling. Brian Tracy calls this the law of expectation. The universe is always listening.

This is why we are encouraged over and over again to get clear on our why. This business is about where we are going, what we are allowing and creating to improve our lives and the lives of others. Writing about and talking about this life that you desire and deserve makes it more real to you. You are aligned with your success and the universe responds accordingly. It is a law. Look ahead. Step into that future reality in present time. Be conscious that the story you tell matches your desires, rather than what you do not want.

* * * * *

The second segment has to do with our thoughts. Thoughts are things. They contain a vibration that determines the reality you experience. If you think that you are a failure in the relationship department, the universe will supply you with ample evidence to support this belief. Do you believe you are worthy of building a large, sustained, profitable, stable organization? Are you 100 percent aligned with knowing that you can create your own economy? Sustained focus on these thoughts plus massive actions will bring results.

We each have some thoughts that we have thought hundreds, perhaps thousands of times. They are incredibly familiar and sometimes we think them unconsciously. These core thoughts reflect core beliefs. A belief is a thought that is repeated enough times until we perceive it as the truth. Each of these thoughts contains a vibration, which is attached to an emotion. We really are what we think.

Here is a little exercise that I have practiced for years. I recommend it as a way to download a new operating system in some of the more important areas of our lives.

Let's imagine a thought that goes something like this: *Oh, I never have enough money.* Have you ever had a thought like this?

How about if you really start paying attention to your thoughts? Get really familiar with these tapes running in your head. With a little practice, you will notice that this thought about not having enough comes with a feeling or emotion attached to it. It is like a vibration, like the "tune" of the thought; it is familiar, but it is not positive. So, negative thought, negative emotion, and negative vibration. How do you know this? You can feel it.

Here is the exercise. Once you notice the thought, when you begin to hear it, turn it off right in the middle. Stop thinking the thought before it is complete. So you get to, *Oh, I never have e-* ... and then stop. Do that for a while. Then you can get so sensitive as to stop after *I never ha-* ... Do that for a while. Then stop after *Oh, I ne-* ...

And then something really magical happens. The vibration, or the emotion connected to the thought, is recognizable *even before the thought forms.* And if you sense that vibration, you can turn to something more positive, something that is more in line with the success you desire. And you go to that thought. With practice, you can stop thinking thoughts that are not aligned with your success, and choose only ones that are. You pivot.

Over time you have replaced the old familiar negative thoughts with new ones that feel great. This helps you create what you desire. It makes the creative process easier and more fun. You have trained and strengthened your mind just as you train and strengthen your body when going to the gym. This is true mental conditioning. You are aligning yourself with your desires.

Now let's combine the two components: the story you tell and the thoughts that you think. Are you telling a story about being a top earner with your company, yet persist in holding thoughts of scarcity around money? Downloading new thoughts and beliefs around abundance will help pave your way to achieving the income of a top earner. Do you pay lip service to time freedom, yet find yourself stressing over time on a daily basis? Allowing yourself to relax into thoughts about the abundance of time will alert the universe to give you more of that. These are golden opportunities, little gems that hold the key for you to get on track, to become the associate you want to attract. Tell a new story. Align your thoughts with good feelings that match your desires. You are well on your way to being aligned with your success. Enjoy the creative process and know that you deserve to live the life of your dreams.

Chapter Nineteen

∽

Flirting with Your Why

Reprinted from *Networking Times Magazine*

During the enrollment process with prospective associates, I always review the person's dreams. As networkers, we should listen carefully to our prospects' wants, don't wants, and needs as fundamental elements in forming this business partnership. I draw an imaginary circle on the table with my hands and point to their dreams as if they are sitting right in front of us. Then I reiterate my offer: I will help you achieve that (for example, quit their job, have more time with their family) if you will help me expand my network by connecting with other people, who also have dreams. Perhaps we should call what we do network *listening* as much as network marketing.

When I first became a professional networker, I was given countless chances to define my why. Everywhere I turned, someone else wanted me to hammer out my purpose for choosing this business model. I spent three days down in San Diego with Denis Waitley, who is a master coach and an expert in helping people discover their inner passions. We went through numerous exercises, exquisitely crafted to help us drill down and identify our goals and desires. I began to feel an internal shift as my personal interpretation of the network marketing lifestyle began to take shape. In this business, defining what it is we are working toward is not an optional line item that we can arbitrarily ignore. We must know where we are headed so we can:

- steer our ship, and
- recognize the landscape to know when we are getting close.

When I returned from this seminar with Dr. Waitley, a fax was waiting for me. My upline mentor had sent me an exercise for helping me identify my why. I thought to myself, *again?* Well, trainable new associate that I was, I reached inside one more time and answered each question to the best of my ability. When I was finished, a huge light bulb went off in my head. I realized that it was just a matter of some time and some effort before all of these dreams and goals became a reality. I began to feel my why moving toward me. It was starting to feel real.

Over the next few years, I continued to write long dissertations detailing my why. Make it vivid, I was told. What do I feel, taste, touch, and smell as I see my future as if it is happening now? After so many tireless hours of dream building, I can now say quite plainly what it is that I have worked toward: *to touch people's lives; to travel and do sports on my own terms; and to leave a legacy for my children.* I now rejoice in both the simplicity of my why, as well as in the manifestation of it.

This summer, while kayaking around Lake Powell, I had another deep realization: I was closing in on the lifestyle of my dreams. *I was flirting with my why.* It is from this perspective that I want to urge anyone who knows what he or she wants to begin to draw his or her dream to himself or herself. It does not serve any of us to hold our dreams at arms length until they are completely manifest. If it is your dream to get a massage every week, start off once a month, and remind yourself that you are getting closer. If it is your dream to donate one thousand dollars per month to your charity of choice, smile and give thanks as you give one hundred dollars. If you want a menagerie of exotic pets, go buy a turtle and name him something like Freedom or Abundance, anything that affirms your ability to realize your dreams.

I have observed among some networkers those whose dreams are so remote that there is no way to identify with them until they are tripping over them. What if there was a scaled-down version of the Big Dream? One of my partners plans to sail around the world with her husband on her network marketing income. On their way to achieving that, they sail around the San Francisco Bay, getting closer with each whitecap that they pass. Conversely, I know a graphic artist who is completely locked into his day job, where he is paid by the hour. His dream is to walk away from a job that he hates and be able to build his own house. Since he rarely looks up to enjoy what life has to offer, I am concerned that he may be missing the piece where he begins to manifest his dream for having taken a tiny taste of it. If he were to take a weekend workshop in some area of home construction, he may get closer than if he keeps his head down. We need to live our why even just a little bit before it has come into full bloom.

Once, many years ago, the founder of Transcendental Meditation, the Maharishi Mahesh Yogi, was asked if enlightenment came gradually or as a click. He responded, "It is a gradual click." I think it is the same way with realizing our why. Ease yourself into it. Let your vision of the network marketing lifestyle creep up on you. It's not black and white, so go out and enjoy the gray. You can energize your belief in your ability to craft this lifestyle-by-design by sidling up to your why. Make it real by living it one page at a time. If that is too ambitious, how about one paragraph at a time? Flirt with your why, and your why might just flirt back with you.

Chapter Twenty

∽

What is Wealth?

Reprinted from the wealth-building section of
a major network marketing Web site

Recently, at a seminar for real estate investors, the presenter said
the most amazing thing: "You know how when you get into your
forties, fifties, sixties, and beyond, and you will probably get sick and
probably have diseases? Well, because of the residual income it produces,
real estate is a great way to make money if you are too sick to work."

How outrageous is it to view getting older as an inevitable journey
into the jaws of disease? Furthermore, what kind of wealth would have
any value whatsoever if the person who has earned it is too ill to enjoy
it? Although assets are necessary to carry anyone through a health crisis,
there is a problem with the speaker's premise because it *presumes* that
we will get sick and be unable to work.

Perhaps this quote by A. J. Reb Materi says it all: "So many people
spend their health gaining wealth, and then have to spend their wealth
to regain their health." John Maxwell, prolific author and founder of
www.injoy.com, refers to the chasing of wealth as sheer folly. He says that
if we put all of our focus on the creation of wealth, to the detriment of

preserving our good health, then in the later years we will find ourselves spending our hard-earned assets in a vain attempt to try to buy back our health. This is hardly a winning formula.

Today I met with a client who pulled up to my office in an eye-catching, head-turning luxury sports car. As we sat down to discuss her health concerns, it became apparent that she took far better care of her car than she did of her body. Her sports car was in great shape but unfortunately for her, her body was falling apart. Something was wrong with this picture. The car/body analogy worked beautifully for her: she enrolled herself into a pro-health disease-prevention program as smoothly as she maneuvered her sporty vehicle along a sharp turn. Now we have someone who is going to be better positioned to enjoy her wealth with a healthy body over time. *This will become one of her truly great investments.* Investing in your health as a sustainable asset will return immeasurable dividends over time.

Marshall Thurber, who is a highly successful lawyer, real estate developer, businessman, educator, scholar, inventor, and public speaker, was asked to define true wealth. His answer was to the point: "The first key piece is health. Take away health and you have no wealth. You have got to start with a sound body."

I share Thurber's passion for creating dual harmony in the arenas of optimal wealth and optimal health. When health and wealth are in balance, the next element in the equation is time. These have been called the three freedoms: time, health, and money. You need all three in equilibrium to live a life of lasting value.

As a health coach, my passion is to support people who are out of alignment with their health by sharing viable resources for creating a body that serves them optimally. We reinforce habits that promote wellness and avoid disease. Teaching wealthy people the *true value* of their health is among the most satisfying jobs I have ever had in thirty-six years in the wellness field. On this subject, Mahatma Gandhi said, "It is health that is real wealth and not pieces of gold and silver." The more people who pursue wealth by investing in their health and longevity (which is the time element), the better off we all are for having those models. It's a paradigm shift, and the guy at the real estate lecture was missing the point.

Epilogue: The realtor now takes his hard-earned assets and invests them in the most valuable treasure he has ever owned: his physical body. His lecture has changed. The world has become a better place as a result of his choice to influence people to have wealth *and* health.

Chapter Twenty One

~

Ten Years, Ten Thousand Hours

This article is to appear in *Networking Times Magazine*

Consider the following occupations: airline pilot, cardiac surgeon, financial planner. If you needed the services in any of these sectors, would you not be more inclined to select a practitioner who had the most experience? Given our druthers, a pilot, surgeon, or planner who has been working in his or her field for a minimum of ten years would seem a better choice than working with a rookie.

Nobody is born knowing his craft. Becoming a master in one's field requires time, practice, and a willingness and commitment to start from scratch in order to eventually excel. Captain "Sully" Sullenberger, the forty-two-year veteran pilot of US Airways who landed a jumbo jet in the Hudson River, said in an interview following the emergency landing, ""I was sure I could do it." This is the voice of experience.

In *Outliers*, a brilliant book about success, Malcolm Gladwell discusses two benchmarks for being able to predict mastery: the number of years and the number of hours someone has devoted to his field. Ten and ten thousand respectively appear to be the magic figures.

Few people who begin a career in network marketing start off seeing themselves still working their businesses over the next decade. However, if we compare the desire to achieve financial freedom with the skills required for such a monumental accomplishment, the question should become, "*Why* not *ten years?*"

THE GIFT OF MISTAKES

Nothing teaches as effectively as learning from our mistakes. We should pay attention to what went wrong with a clear intent to improve as a result of what we learned. I have had two long careers that spanned over ten years, the second being network marketing. In both careers, when the five year bell rang I had the distinct experience that I was no longer working in the dark. When the clock struck ten years, again, I experienced a shift for having run out of major mistakes that had peppered my experience in the early years. Mistakes will provide us with lessons that are critical for developing confidence and proficiency. We should avoid mistakes; we should also respect them for the teachers that they are. It seems a shame to me to make mistakes and then not to stick around to benefit from the lessons that they provide.

MAKING MONEY VERSUS CREATING WEALTH

Some people come to network marketing and appear to defy the laws of nature as they fly up the ranks of their company's leadership levels. These breathtaking feats are an inspiration to others who take longer to hit the mark. However, there is something incredibly important to remember: the people who make fast money might not be the same as those who create freedom. The later takes time, years in fact. There is nothing wrong with being a super star from the beginning. But if those efforts go up in flames due to unwillingness on the part of the associate to solidify what was built, then network marketing begins to look like a job in which the income stops when the work comes to a halt. We promulgate freedom. How many of us stick around long enough for *that* golden egg?

FLYING HOURS

When pilots discuss their experience, they talk about number of hours in the cockpit in the air. A pilot who has been flying for five years can have more or less practical experience than another pilot who has been flying for, say, ten years. In network marketing, we espouse the benefits of a business that the average person can do in his spare time. To be authentic, we should add that working this business in our spare time *over time*, is the magic formula. Something that is as precious as freedom should not be cheapened by claims that anyone can do this in his sleep. Giving a presentation is an example. It is important to distinguish between the duration of time a distributor has been presenting, for example, "for a few years," versus the number of actual presentations someone has given. One could expedite the "ten thousand hours" by giving more presentations in less time thus improving more rapidly than someone who gives fewer presentation over a longer period of time.

MIRACLES HAPPEN

Anyone who has worked in this business faithfully has inevitably experienced the ups and downs that come with the territory. Over time, the ratio of challenges to rewards shifts. Some of the most magical things happen only as a result of sustained effort. After ten years, people who have been watching you may decide that it is time to work with you. Among these people are a couple of individual or even one person who could help you take your business to a whole new level. For anyone who quits early in the game, she runs the risk of not being able to answer the call of someone who wasn't ready before, but is now. This is the same for distributors in your organization who fell asleep at the wheel. Some of these individuals will only come back to the business if someone is there holding the fort when they lift their heads to be counted. Frequently, these people are particularly valuable because they may have been loyal product users, often for a long time, even years. When they decide to get involved, their belief is even higher than someone who recently got involved. These people are great assets to your organization. They are your prize for being among those who faithfully stayed the course. Those who drop by just for a visit will never receive them.

Recommended Reading and Listening

NETWORK MARKETING, FINANCES, AND BUSINESS

Adler, Jordan. *Beach Money* (2008) (available at *www.beachmoney.com*)

Allen, Robert G. *The One Minute Millionaire (2002); Multiple Streams of Internet Income* (2006) (available at *www.robertgallen.com*)

Bach, David. *Start Late, Finish Rich* (2006); *The Automatic Millionaire* (2004) (available at *www.barnesandnoble.com*)

Barrett, Tom. *Dare to Dream, Work to Win* (1998) (available at *www.daretodream.net*)

Canfield, Jack and Janet Switzer. *The Success Principles: How to Get from Where You Are to Where You Want to Be* (2006) (available at *www.amazon.com*)

Chandler, Steve and Scott Richardson. *100 Ways to Motivate Others* (2008) (available at *www.amazon.com*)

Clayton-Law, Fiona. *Wealth Creation—What Your Accountant Doesn't Tell You* (2001) (available at *www.amazon.com*)

Failla, Don. *The 45 Second Presentation That Will Change Your Life* (2006) (available at *www.amazon.com*)

Fenton, Richard, and Andrea Waltz. *Go for No!* (2007) (available at *www.amazon.com*)

Fogg, John Milton. *The Greatest Networker in the World* (1997) (available at *www.barnesandnoble.com*)

Hicks, Jerry and Esther. *Money and the Law of Attraction: Learning to Attract Wealth, Health, and Happiness* (2008) (available at *www.abraham-hicks.com*)

Kiyosaki, Robert. *The Business School for People Who Like Helping People* (2002); *Cash Flow Quadrant* (2002) (available at *www.richdad.com*)

Mulvaney, Maureen. *The Women's Millionaire Club* (2009) (available at *www.mgmsuperstar.com*)

Oliver, Michael. *How to Sell Network Marketing Without Fear, Anxiety or Losing Your Friends!* (2002) (available at *www.amazon.com*)

Patterson, Kerry, Joseph Grenny, David Maxfield, Ron McMillan, and Al Switzler. *Influencer: The Power to Change Anything* (2007) (available at *www.amazon.com*)

Poe, Richard. *Wave 4: Network Marketing in the 21st Century* (2000) (available at *www.amazon.com*)

Tracy, Brian. *The Answer* (CD) (available at *www.briantracy.com*. Recommended daily quotes via e-mail)

Thomas, Dr. Stanley. *The Millionaire Next Door* (1998); *The Millionaire Mind* (2001); and *The Women Millionaire Next Door* (2004) (available at *www.amazon.com*)

Watts, Dr. Lloyd. *The Flow of Time and Money: How to Create a Full and Prosperous Life* (2008) (available at *www.lloydwatts.com*)

Yarnell, Mark. *Your First Year in Network Marketing: Overcome Your Fears, Experience Success, and Achieve Your Dreams!* (1998) (available at *www.amazon.com*)

Professional and Personal Development

Allen Johnson, Lynn. *Getting Out of Your Own Way* (2007) (available at *www.unitogether.com*)

Arbinger Institute. *Leadership and Self Deception: Getting Out of the Box* (2000) (available at *www.amazon.com*)

Burg, Bob and John David Mann. *The Go Giver* (2007) (available at *www.amazon.com*)

Canfield, Jack, Mark Victor Hansen, and Les Hewitt. *The Power of Focus* (2000) (available at *www.amazon.com*)

Canfield, Jack and Mark Victor Hansen. *The Aladdin Factor* (1995) (available at *www.amazon.com*)

Eker, T. Harv. *Secrets of the Millionaire Mind* (2005) (available at *www.amazon.com*)

Hicks, Jerry and Esther. *Ask and It is Given* (2005); *The Law of Attraction* (2006); *The Astonishing Power of Emotions* (2008) (available at *www.amazon.com*)

Klemmer, Brian. *The Compassionate Samurai: Being Extraordinary in an Ordinary World* (2009) (available at *www.klemmer.com*)

Leonard, George. *Mastery* (1992) (available at *www.amazon.com*)

Lofholm, Eric. *How to Sell in the New Economy* (2010) (available at *http://www.ericlofholm.com/products/*)

Mortensen, Kurt W. *Maximum Influence: The 12 Universal Laws of Power Persuasion* (2004) (available at *www.amazon.com*)

Olson, Jeff. *The Slight Edge* (2005) (available at *www.amazon.com*)

Patterson, Kerry, Joseph Grenny, David Maxfield, Ron McMillan, and Al Switzler. *Crucial Conversations* (2002) (available at *www.amazon.com*)

Schwartz, David. *The Magic of Thinking Big* (1987) (available at *www.amazon.com*)

Waitley, Denis. *The Psychology of Winning* (1986) (available at *www.deniswaitley.com*)

HEALTH AND NUTRITION

Bisset, Jenny, Anne Forte, and Tannis Kristjanson. *Slender with a Blender* (2009) (available at *www.slenderwithablender.com*)

McNamara, Dr. Ladd. *The Cholesterol Conspiracy* (2004) (available at *www.laddmcnamara.com*)

MacWilliam, Lyle. *Comparative Guide to Nutritional Supplements* (professional and consumer edition) (available at *www.comparativeguide.com*)

Northrup, Dr. Christiane. *The Wisdom of Menopause, 2ⁿᵈ Edition* (2006) (available at *www.amazon.com*)

Sinatra, Dr. Stephen. *The Coenzyme Q10 Phenomenon* (1998) (available at *www.amazon.com*)

Strand, Dr. Ray. *Medical Evidence that Demands a Verdict* (2002); *Preventing Diabetes* (2006); *Fibromyalgia/Chronic Fatigue; What Your Doctor Doesn't Tell You About Nutritional Medicine May Be Killing You* (2002); *Releasing Fat* (2003); *Healthy for Life* (2005) (available at *www.raystrand.com*)

Wentz, Dr. Myron. *Invisible Miracles* (2003); *A Mouth Full of Poison* (2006) (available at *www.unitogether.com*)

Wood Dr. Christine. *How to Get Kids to Eat Great and Love It.* (available at *www.kidseatgreat.com*)

About the Author

Rosie Bank is the founder of Manifesting Vision International, a global network marketing organization that trains women and men to succeed as home-based business owners. Rosie is also a health coach whose emphasis is teaching people how to live more successfully in their bodies. She has been in the wellness field since 1973 and is the author of *Yoga for Rolfers, Movement Teachers and Their Clients, Lessons in Embodiment,* and *Bodies, Health, and Consciousness.*

As a regular contributor to *Networking Times Magazine,* Rosie was recently featured as "Master Networker." Rosie is a graduate of the Klemmer and Associates leadership seminar and is an active member and officer of Toastmasters International. She has a B.A. in Spanish from the University of Colorado, Boulder.

Rosie practices her craft by leading a lifestyle that focuses on a healthy diet, optimal nutrition, and exercise. Rosie lives in Foster City, California. For more information, please visit www.rosiebank.com and www.you-inc.biz.